The Disconnected Generation

Saving Our Youth from Self-Destruction

Josh McDowell

W PUBLISHING GROUP™

www.wpublishinggroup.com

A Division of Thomas Nelson, Inc.
www.ThomasNelson.com

Unless otherwise indicated, Scripture quotations used in this book are from the Holy Bible, New International Version. Copyright ©1973, 1978, 1984, International Bible Society. Used by permission of Zondervan Bible Publishers.

Other Scripture references are from the following sources:

The Living Bible (TLB), copyright © 1971 by Tyndale House Publishers, Wheaton, Ill. Used by permission.

J. B. Phillips: The New Testament in Modern English, Revised Edition (Phillips). Copyright © J. B. Phillips 1958, 1960, 1972. Used by permission of Macmillan Publishing Co., Inc.

The New American Standard Bible ® (NASB), © copyright The Lockman Foundation 1960, 1962, 1963, 1968, 1971, 1972, 1973, 1975, 1977. Used by permission.

The Holy Bible, New Living Translation, copyright © 1996. Used by permission of Tyndale House Publishers, Inc., Wheaton, Illinois 60189. All rights reserved.

Library of Congress Cataloging-in-Publication Data

McDowell, Josh.

    The disconnected generation / by Josh McDowell

      p. cm.

    Includes bibliographical references.

    ISBN 0-8499-4077-X (tp)

    1. Parent and teenager—United States. 2. Parenting—United States. 3. Parent and teenager—Religious aspects—Christianity. 4. Parenting—Religious aspects. 5. Teenagers—United States—Family relationships. 6. Teenagers—Religious life—United States. I. Title.

HQ799.15 .M377 2000

306.874—dc21
                                        00-036483

                                            CIP

Printed in the United States of America

2 3 4 PHX 9 8 7 6

Contents

This book is dedicated to all the parents who grieved over the events of April 20, 1999. The school shooting in Littleton, Colorado, shook the world and woke up many to the fact that our culture is in crisis. In the weeks and months that followed the tragedy, I struggled with the question, What can be done to bring about lasting change? Beyond that, I asked what more can *I* do? Out of a nation's tragedy has come a powerful message of hope and change. *The Disconnected Generation,* along with the PROJECT 911 family of products, is my gift to the parents and families of Columbine.

Acknowledgments

A book like this simply could not have been published without the contributions of a number of dedicated and talented people. I would like to thank the following individuals for their efforts:

Dick Day has been my mentor and dearest friend from my earliest days of seminary. Dick, to a great degree, has been the content source for this book's relational connecting points. I have drawn from Dick's life and message for many years, and he has enriched my own life and family beyond measure.

David Ferguson has contributed much to my own life as well as to this book. David and his wife, Teresa, direct Intimate Life Ministries in Austin, Texas. Many of the principles taught by Intimate Life are reflected in the PROJECT 911 family of resources. (For more information on Intimate Life Ministries, see pages 223–26)

Ed Stewart participated as a coauthor with me on this book. Ed's gift for writing is present in each sentence, paragraph, and page. This book carries what we affectionately refer to as the "Ed touch," which will inspire, challenge, and enlighten the reader.

Dave Bellis, my associate of twenty-three years, labored over every page with Ed and me, provided the book's focused theme, cowrote many of the chapters with us, and cowrote, designed, and coordinated the entire PROJECT 911 family of resources.

(For more information on the PROJECT 911 resources, see pages 232–35)

My wife, Dottie, critiqued the manuscript and contributed to many of the illustrations in this book. She has also partnered with me for twenty-nine fabulous years of marriage.

My daughter, Kelly McDowell, provided much of the secondary research on the medical development of the brain.

Christy Karassev, my administrative assistant, copied, faxed, and cut and pasted more pages in the early draft of this book than she cares to mention.

Deborah Jackson critiqued the book and provided valuable insights to its contents.

Becky Bellis retyped the final draft of the manuscript.

Jennifer Stair provided invaluable assistance not only with her editing expertise, but also with her efforts to help us broaden the book's appeal.

Joey Paul of Word Publishing not only championed the PROJECT 911 family of resources throughout Word, but he also has been both an inspiration and a dedicated partner with us in publishing these many resources.

I appreciate and respect the contribution of each of these people, and I'm grateful to God for their involvement with this project.

—Josh D. McDowell
Dallas, Texas

PART 1

The Generational Disconnection

CHAPTER 1

The Disconnected
Path of Self-Destruction

I cannot remember feeling more sad or heartsick than when I heard each of the following news stories for the first time. Perhaps they hit you the same way:

- In the quiet town of West Paducah, Kentucky, fourteen-year-old Michael Carneal opens fire on a group of teenagers circled in prayer, leaving three of them dead.

- In Pearl, Mississippi, sixteen-year-old Luke Woodham shoots his mother to death then goes to his high school and starts firing, killing three and wounding seven.

- Mitchell Johnson, thirteen, and Andrew Golden, eleven, trip a fire alarm in their Jonesboro, Arkansas, junior high school. Once their classmates are outside, the boys start shooting at them, killing four students and a teacher.

- Gunpowder, crude bombs, and computer disks with bomb-making information are found in the homes of three fourteen-year-old Wimberly, Texas, boys accused of plotting an assault at their junior high school.

- After murdering his parents at home, fifteen-year-old Springfield, Oregon, student Kip Kinkel sprays his school cafeteria with gunfire. Twenty-four students are hit; two die.

- Eric Harris, eighteen, and Dylan Klebold, seventeen, go on a killing rampage at Columbine High School in Littleton, Colorado. When twelve students and a teacher are dead and twenty-three students are wounded, the boys conclude the terror with their own suicides.

Since writing these chilling lines, I suspect that even more communities like West Paducah, Springfield, and Littleton have experienced similar carnage and tragedy. Youth rage and murder are escalating at a shocking rate, leading to more shootings, bombings, and killings by young people in school hallways and on quiet suburban streets.

Alarming surveys among teenagers show:

- 80 percent of students at a Midwestern middle school had bullied their peers to some degree in the past thirty days.

- 19 percent of students say they have been hit, slapped, or kicked while at school.

- 25 percent of students indicate they are afraid another student will harm them.[1]

- More than half of American teens believe a murderous rampage could erupt at their schools.[2]

Romans 3:16–17 aptly describes these news stories and statistics: "Destruction and misery are in their paths, and the path of peace have they not known" (NASB). It is only natural to ask why. What causes our teenagers to lash out at their parents, teachers, and peers with lethal violence? What has happened in our culture to allow mere children to become so callous and violent? An even more alarming question is, Will our own young people get caught up in this juvenile mayhem?

On the surface, the proliferation of violence in the media—particularly interactive media in the form of killing-based video games—appears to contribute to the violent acting out of some of our youth.

When the U.S. military realized that fewer than 20 percent of American soldiers fired their weapons during World War II, they concluded that soldiers needed to increase their firing rate to enhance the killing rate. The U.S. Army learned, according to Lt. Col. David Grossman, author of *On Killing: The Psychological Cost of Learning to Kill in War and Society*, that shooting at mere bull's-eyes in practice did not result in the soldiers' firing weapons in battle. But directing the soldiers' firing practice at man-shaped outlines numbed their consciences and made killing a reflex reaction.

According to Grossman, a psychologist who formerly taught the psychology of war at West Point, today's modern video games are even more effective in causing a person to overcome the aversion to shooting. He states:

> The more realistic touches in video games help blur the boundary between fantasy and reality—i.e., guns carefully molded after real ones, accurate-looking wounds, screams, and other sound effects, even the recoil of a heavy rifle.[3]

Grossman goes on to contend that the traits of killing games are evident in some of the recent shootings:

> Michael Carneal, the schoolboy shooter in Paducah, Ky., showed the effects of video-game lessons in killing. Carneal coolly shot nine times, hitting eight people, five of them in the head or neck. Head shots pay a bonus in many video games. . . .We have to start worrying about what we are putting into the minds of our young. Pilots train on flight simulators, drivers on driving simulators, and now we have our children on murder simulators.[4]

But there is something more behind youth rage, murder, and mayhem than bloody video games and movies. I posed questions about our violent youth culture back in 1994 in my book *Right from Wrong*.[5] A response from journalist Rowland Nethaway bears repeating:

> Adults have always complained about their youth, but this is different. There have always been wild and rebellious kids who would go off the track and do something wrong. Many of today's youth don't seem to know right from wrong. Children are robbing, maiming and killing on whims, and with no pity and no remorse.[6]

I agree with Nethaway. A significant part of the problem is the disappearance of moral absolutes from our culture. Youth violence thrives in a moral vacuum. When kids don't have a personal value system that distinguishes between right and wrong, there is nothing to prevent them from venting their anger and frustration through violence and cold disregard for human life. Restoring moral absolutes to the fabric of our families and society is key to curbing the destructive trends among our youth.

To that end, I have taken the Right from Wrong campaign across our country for the past several years. I accepted the challenge to equip churches and families to resist the erosion of biblical values and help our children determine right from wrong. My team and I have traveled to four continents and more than 160 cities, resulting in an estimated sixty thousand churches embracing the message of moral absolutes. We have developed thirty-two different resources and taught hundreds of thousands of parents and youth a biblical, practical

> Restoring moral absolutes to the fabric of our families and society is key to curbing the destructive trends among our youth.

blueprint for understanding and implementing moral absolutes in their lives and relationships.

If I felt the need, I would do it all over again. But as important as it is to instill in our young people a personal right-from-wrong values system, moral values are only one key dimension of the answer to today's youth crisis. Teaching our young people right from wrong is vital to the solution, but it is not the entire solution. We must also take steps to protect them from becoming immersed in a culture that glorifies violence and illicit sex. We must allow them to experience the love and nurture of a caring family. Our kids must learn what it means to honor and respect people and property.

Yet I believe there is a deeper crying need among our youth that must be addressed as we restore moral absolutes and stand against a sin-filled world. If I were asked to identify the core reason that our young people are succumbing to the lure of a godless culture and lashing out with rage, I would say it is that they feel alone, disconnected, and unsure of who they really are. Many young people, even those from good Christian homes, feel disconnected and alienated from their parents, from adults in general, and from society as a whole. Recent scientific studies, my personal research, and my interaction with thousands of young people confirm that our kids today

> Teaching our young people right from wrong is vital to the solution, but it is not the entire solution.

are disconnected from most adults and lack a sense of personal identity and purpose. This alienation from adults and fuzzy sense of identity cause them to feel adrift in a hostile world. That's why I call them the disconnected generation.

The relational disconnection that young people feel today is both frightening and emotionally painful to them, and much of the antisocial behaviors they exhibit—including extremes like West Paducah, Jonesboro, and Columbine—are the result. In order to reach the disconnected generation, we must first understand their makeup and why they feel so painfully disconnected and alone.

ON-LINE BUT DISCONNECTED

The disconnected generation is in a population group some have referred to as the "echo boomers," born between 1977 and 1994. Some call them the "millennials." Those born after 1983 are sometimes called the "mosaics." Today's adolescents are primarily the offspring of baby boomers. The teenage population is more than twenty-two million strong. They are perhaps the richest, most populous, best educated, and most physically fit generation in history.[7] Our young people are growing up in a prosperous society with unprecedented career opportunities and access to a virtually limitless amount of information. More than one-third of today's teenagers are connected to the Internet, and it is projected that 70 percent will be cruising along the information superhighway by 2003.[8]

Today's youth are logging on to the Internet for more than just information and entertainment. Increasing numbers of young people are using e-mail and chat rooms in an attempt to connect socially with others. Yet people who are seeking emotional and relational connections on-line are finding electronic relationships unfulfilling, a cheap substitute for in-person friendships and interaction. A study out of Carnegie Mellon University in Pittsburgh reveals that the more hours a person spends on the Internet, the more depressed, stressed, and lonely he or she feels.[9] Hill Walker, codirector of the Institute on Violence and Destructive Behavior, calls the results of the new communication technologies "almost a virtual reality without adults."[10]

The high-tech devices that allow our kids to connect electronically with people around the world may also be encouraging them to disconnect relationally with people at home. In a rapidly increasing number of homes, students have their own computers, modems, and phone lines. And since many homes are also equipped with PCs for Mom and Dad, kids and their parents spend more time staring at their monitors than they do interacting with one another. As wonderful as computers may be for many tasks, they can be insidious contributors to the disconnected generation. As kids spend hours surfing the Internet, chatting with people on-line, and playing computer games, they have less time to interact with others, specifically their parents and other significant adults. Adults who are similarly preoccupied with the Internet, careers, social activities, or church commitments are equally at risk of disconnecting from their kids.

Every major sociological study during the last fifteen years that cross-tabulates human relationships—or the lack of them—with human behavior reveals that the more disconnected a person is relationally, the more prone he or she is to engage in antisocial behavior. Two major studies I commissioned of churched youth, the first in 1987 and the second in 1994, reveal that the closer youth are to their parents relationally, the less at risk they are for unacceptable behavior. And yet the sobering statistics underscore the mounting disconnection and loneliness in this generation:

> The more disconnected a person is relationally, the more prone he or she is to engage in antisocial behavior.

- Almost half of today's young people have lived through their parents' divorce.

- 63 percent of youth live in households in which both parents work outside the home.

- Only 25 percent of teenagers say their mothers are always home when they return from school.

- 98 percent of teenagers spend eleven hours per week watching TV.

- Teenagers spend an average of three and one-half hours alone every day.[11]

We should not be surprised that the generation which suffers through parental divorce, comes home to an empty house, spends an inordinate amount of time alone, and sits for hours in front of a TV or computer monitor is also the generation that feels disconnected from adults and exhibits at-risk behavior. When young people's painful sense of aloneness is not adequately dealt with, their anger and fear may escalate into violence and tragedy.

I receive thousands of cards and letters from young people every year. My eyes light up when I read one like this, which I received recently from a high-school girl. Here's an excerpt:

> Dear Josh,
>
> My parents are both Christians and have been for many years. I have been raised in church all my life. My parents have been together for twenty years this July. They are the most loving, understanding people God could have given me as parents. I don't know what I would do without my wonderful parents. They are the greatest!

But for every encouraging letter like this, I must get a dozen or more heartbreaking letters from young men and women who feel disconnected from one or both of their parents. Here are some of the sad words kids have written to me:

> I am so lonely I can hardly stand it. I want to be special to someone, but there's no one who cares about me. I can't remember anyone touching me, smiling at me, or wanting to be with me. I feel so empty inside.

•••

It's like I have a heavy heart and this burden upon my back, but I don't know what it is. There is something in me that makes me want to cry, and I don't even know what it is.

●●●

In my life, I haven't gone through much, but I have always had a strong feeling of loneliness. In fact, yesterday I saw a guy my age by the lake with his head in his hands. I went over to him, and we talked awhile. I found out that we both have been filled with loneliness and confusion over the years.

●●●

I'm going to be sixteen on July 1. I was eleven years old when my real dad molested me. Because of that I have tried to kill myself three times. I closed up. I hated people. I'm saved now, but I need to learn to love again. I'm tired of being alone, but I'm so afraid to love.

Your students may not be on the verge of violence, but you may be shocked to learn how disconnected they possibly feel.

THE OLD GENERATION GAP

The infamous generation gap, the social and emotional distance separating adults from their children, has always existed to some degree. It is natural for each new generation to want to establish a unique identity apart from their parents. But when massive societal changes occur within a short period of time, the generation gap widens. And perhaps no generation in history has witnessed as rapid and expansive changes in such a short period of time as that of today's adolescents.

Think about this: The younger generation has all been born since Ronald Reagan became president of the United States. Most of them probably never bought a new vinyl record or watched a drive-in movie. Many can't remember a world without AIDS. Most are too young to remember the fall of communism. They can't imagine a world without computers, video games, or the Internet. The world has changed rapidly in their short lifetimes, and today's adolescents reflect those changes.

Consider for a moment the contrast between the baby boomers and today's youth:

Baby Boomers	Millennials
Color TV	Internet
Working Fathers	Absent Fathers
At-home Mothers	Day Care
Women Employees	Women Managers
LPs	CDs
Rock-'n'-Roll	Hip-hop
Long Hair	Body Piercing
"Free" Sex	"Safe" Sex[12]

Ethnically, this new generation is more diverse than the baby boomers. They are the first generation to claim computer technology as a birthright. For the most part, they have not actually rebelled against their parents; they simply feel distant from them.

A New Cultural Language Gap

A cultural language gap also distances adults from youth, and many adults are simply unaware of it. In fact, most young people speak a totally different language from that of their parents and other adults. I'm not talking about some homes in which the parents speak Spanish or Russian or Chinese while their children speak English. I'm not even talking about the slang terms kids use today that many adults don't understand. I'm talking about adults and youth using a common vocabulary with different definitions, completely unaware that such differences exist. As the distance between adults and youth widens, our young people are forming a tight-knit community of their own with a language all their own. Can you see why adults and young people with a different language might not connect with one another?

> Most young people speak a totally different language from that of their parents and other adults.

For example, sixteen-year-old Jason has locked horns with his father over his "need" for a part-time job. Listen to Jason and his dad to see if you can discern the origin of the cultural language gap, something his father doesn't even realize exists.

Jason's view:
It's not that I hate my parents or anything. I just wish they could understand me. I mean, there's this issue of having a job. Dad is always on my case about studying hard and getting good grades. He thinks having a car and a good sound system and the right clothes are not important. He's always putting me down for wanting to make money and have nice things. Well, that's

who I am, and Dad just can't handle it. And Mom is always saying I'm too eager to "store up treasures on earth," whatever that means. She says it's better to be rich spiritually instead of materially. That may work for Mom and Dad, but my friends and I believe you can have both. My parents just don't get it. They are so judgmental. They don't give me any credit for being who I am. It's like they're rejecting their own son. I have no freedom. They just keep saying, "You can make decisions like an adult when you start acting like an adult." Well, if acting like an adult means being like them, I don't think I want to be one.

Dad's view:
Jason is a good kid. I know he's a little hardheaded at times, but he'll pull out of it eventually. He really needs to get off this kick of getting a job so he can buy all the CDs he wants. He needs to seek God's kingdom first. I am trying to teach biblical values to him, but he thinks his mother and I are pretty tough on him at times. I'm sure he will eventually realize that what we're doing is best for him. He needs constructive criticism and healthy correction just like I did growing up. Sure, he's a little distant now, but he'll come around. I know I did with my folks.

Can you see why Jason and his parents are not connecting? Dad and Mom consider their son to be "a little distant," but Jason's response is much more serious. His parents are attempting to correct their son's behavior in hopes of equipping him for a better life. But in Jason's mind, they are rejecting him as a person by disapproving of his behavior. In his parents' view, they are doing the loving thing for their son. In Jason's view, they are disconnecting from him relationally.

Why does Jason perceive things so differently from his parents? Because most of the input he receives from public education, advertising, movies, TV, secular music, and his peers is colored by the modern cultural doctrine of postmodernism. Postmodernism is a worldview characterized by the belief that truth is *created* rather than *discovered*. Jason's values are being subtly shaped by postmodernism, but his parents' values reflect those of their own generation. In Jason's world, the words *moral judgment* have been redefined. The terminology is often the same, but the definitions of those terms are very different between the generations.

For example, postmodernism asserts that an individual's identity is inseparable from what he or she does, thinks, and believes. Thus today's kids are influenced to believe that who they are is essentially equal to what they believe and do. So if your opinions, instructions, or methods of discipline somehow clash with what your young people think or do, they may tend to think you are disparaging them. And if you suggest that their behavior is wrong, they may feel, as Jason does, that you are judging them. If you criticize their friends or fashions, they are likely to take the criticism personally. The word *acceptance* has been redefined to this generation.

> So today's kids are influenced to believe that who they are is essentially equal to what they believe and do.

The word *tolerance* also means something different to this generation than it does to you. The postmodern culture is subtly teaching students that people who do not wholeheartedly accept the beliefs or lifestyles of others are intolerant, judgmental bigots—and no one wants a relationship with a bigot! But what does a young person like Jason do when the "intolerant, judgmental bigots" happen to be his disapproving parents? Since most kids are still largely dependent on their parents, Jason will probably not "divorce" his parents and run away. But he will likely distance himself from them relationally because he senses that they are rejecting him.

Consider another word that is being subtly redefined by the postmodern culture: *truth*. As a Bible-believing adult, you undoubtedly accept some things to be absolutely and universally true; that is, true for all people, in all places, and at all times. You also accept that these absolutes are determined by God and communicated to us through His Word. It is this view of truth and morality that formed the basis for much of western civilization up through the modern age. You and your contemporaries were raised on this value.

However, the present generation, the first to grow up in a postmodern age, does not universally accept the existence of objective truth. Since truth to a postmodern world is *created* rather than *discovered,* each culture determines its own truth that is true only in and for that culture. Postmodernists contend that anyone who claims to hold an objective truth that unfavorably judges the values, beliefs, or lifestyle of another person is intolerant and bigoted. This is why Jason is unwilling to accept his parents' values. He is being conditioned to create his own truth, a lifestyle that works for him even though it may clash with the values of his parents.

Since today's youth have grown up under this influence to some degree, they may discuss key issues using the same terms you use—but with different definitions. These differences and misunderstandings may encourage a relational disconnection between you and your youth. Consider how the terms in the following chart are defined differently from generation to generation:

Word	Your Understanding (Adult Culture)	Postmodern Understanding (Youth Culture)
Tolerance	Accepting others without agreeing with or sharing their beliefs or lifestyle choices	Accepting that every individual's beliefs, values, lifestyles, and truth claims are equal.
Respect	Giving due consideration to others.	Wholeheartedly approving of others' beliefs or lifestyle choices.
Acceptance	Embracing people for who they are, not necessarily for what they say or do.	Endorsing and even praising others for their beliefs and lifestyle choices.
Moral Judgments	Certain things are morally right and wrong, as determined by God.	We have no right to judge another person's view or behavior.
Personal Preference	Preferences of color, food, clothing style, hobbies, etc., are personally determined.	Preferences of sexual behaviors, value systems, and beliefs are personally determined.
Personal Rights	Everyone has the right to be treated justly under the law.	Everyone has the right to do what they believe is best for them.
Freedom	Being free to do what you know you ought to do.	Being able to do anything you want to do.
Truth	An absolute standard of right and wrong.	Whatever is right for you.

How Disconnection Turns to Isolation

It is true that the generation gap accounts for a measure of the relational disconnection young people feel today. And the influences of the postmodern culture on this generation make connecting with kids incredibly challenging and difficult. But even with these forces at work, the distance and loneliness our youth feel would not be permanently destructive if parents, youth workers, pastors, and Christian educators would prayerfully counter the culture and build lasting relational connections with their kids. The aloofness and distance that some adults might pass off as a youthful phase or temporary adolescent identity crisis are fast becoming a cultural condition. When our youth's sense of alienation and aloneness is not immediately and adequately addressed, and when they are left to themselves to find themselves, the distance they feel from adults becomes a relational isolation gap.

Many members of this generation are isolated emotionally as well as relationally. They feel lost, not knowing who they really are. A bright Christian student named Danny said something to me some time ago that represents far too many of our youth: "Sometimes I feel so alone, like no one cares. My folks live in their own world, and I live in mine. It didn't always seem to be this way. I know it sounds crazy, but I want them to leave me alone, and yet I want to be a part of their lives. Most of the time they do leave me alone, and it gets pretty lonely." When you hear the desperation of kids like Danny, you can better understand why young people reach out so much for each other. You can see why gangs are attractive—they help close the isolation gap that exists between kids and the adult world.

Traveling tens of thousands of miles across the country and around the world each year, I hear countless hundreds of young people share a sense of isolation with me. Our kids need strong relational connections today to find their way in the world and to escape the riptide of loneliness pulling them toward self-destruction.

Sadly, however, hundreds of parents and youth leaders have told me that they struggle to know their kids and often fail to connect with them at a deep, personal level. I hear caring yet frightened adults say, "Josh, I'm afraid the culture is going to capture my kids." These are good parents and youth workers who love their kids and desperately want to enter their world, to connect with them, and to let them know they are loved for who they are. They just struggle in doing so.

Obviously, we want to protect our kids from the negative influences and consequences of a godless culture. The postmodern culture threatens to undermine our students' faith and moral character. Yet we are misguided if we focus our energies solely on changing our kids' behavior or militantly resisting the godless culture. It is important to understand the damaging influences of our age, and it is vital that young people make right choices in life. But the real battlefields are the very hearts of today's youth.

> The postmodern culture threatens to undermine our students' faith and moral character.

Yes, you want your kids to *live* well and to *behave* well. But they will continue to struggle with loneliness and emptiness until you convince them that they are loved for the unique people they are. This may be an old cliché, but it's true: Your kids won't care how much you know until they know how much you care. Parents, I know you love your children. Youth workers, I know you care about the kids in your youth group. Pastors and Sunday-school teachers, I know you are concerned about the disconnected generation, and your hearts ache with mine over the senseless savagery that has erupted in places like Pearl, Mississippi; Springfield, Oregon; and Littleton, Colorado. If you did not care, you would not be doing what you are doing to find some answers, including reading this book.

The real challenge before us is learning how to enter our students' sometimes complex and confusing world and make relational connections at a deep, emotional level that no cultural influence will be able to destroy. That's what I want for my own four kids and for the tens of thousands of kids around the world I minister to each year. I'm sure that's what you want too. And that's what this book is all about.

The first step in this process is learning to understand and to identify with the struggles our kids face in the preteen and teen world. The closing paragraphs in this chapter will launch us in that direction.

Allow me to present what I believe is a representative voice of the millennial generation. These words, spoken on behalf of the disconnected generation, reveal what today's youth inwardly long for, even though they may not know how to describe it. As you read these words, I encourage you to listen for the heart cry of a young person you know—your son, your daughter, a young person in your youth group, Sunday-school class, or classroom. In reality, the young person closest to you probably shares the deep inner longing to be more closely connected to you.

WORLDS APART: A MILLENNIAL'S VIEW

We're different from you. We live in a different world and represent a different generation. We both live busy lives. And even though we don't spend a lot of time relating to each other, we do spend enough time together for us to learn what you're really afraid of. You're afraid we won't get good enough grades in school. You're definitely afraid that we're having sex or that we soon will be or that peer pressure will lead us into drugs, alcohol, or a gang. And we sort of understand your fears. Your urgent message is pretty clear to us: "Stay out of trouble and get good grades."

But do you know what? All that stuff doesn't really scare us much. In fact, we would like you to think that we already know a lot of things and are confident about who we are and what we want to become. We want you to be proud of us, but at the same time we want to be our own people, different but really important to you.

I know it may sound a little weird, but our world is full of weird people going through weird stages. We are experiencing a confusing time that you may call a phase, but we're afraid it may never end. Really, we're kind of afraid that you're even afraid of us. Like you're afraid because you don't think you know us anymore and maybe you can't trust us, or you're afraid we no longer want to be a part of you.

But deep inside, we long for you to break through our masks and know the real us—to value and trust us. We do want to feel connected to you, like we really belong. I know at times it doesn't seem like that's what we're saying, with the strange things we do and say. But we're really saying that we feel disconnected, like we don't know who we are, and we're frightened that we'll never find out.

You know what's weird? We may not be so different after all, because I think you want that connection too. I think both of us want to need each other. Deep down, we really do want you to enter our world and help us figure out who we are. That's what we're saying, only maybe we're saying it in a strange way. That's because we're confused and struggling.

It seems like we are being measured all the time in terms of numbers and scores and performances that always seem just out of our reach. Each morning when the alarm goes off, our masks go on. We put on our clothes and jewelry and those attitudes of ours to hide our fears. A lot of times we get into sports or clubs or studies or boyfriends or girlfriends or something else just so we can be ourselves or find ourselves or maybe even lose ourselves.

But do you know what? Most of us aren't finding ourselves. That's frustrating, and it hurts. Many of us have become angry inside. Most of us don't even know why we're angry. For that matter, most of us don't even realize that we have no sense of identity. But underneath it all, we feel the pain of being disconnected and alone in our own world, and just below the surface there's this seething anger.

You may not relate to our anger, but perhaps you can understand what we're feeling. Because you probably know what it's like to want to be loved for just being yourself without any strings attached. We think you can identify with that inner ache that longs for someone just to cry with you when you've been hurt or to hang in there with you when you've blown it. Wouldn't it be great to hear the words, "I'm so proud of you for just being you"? And wouldn't it be something to know that people think you are okay even when your actions aren't always perfect?

Here's something else that would be great: We would love for you to look past our clothes and our music, to peer behind our masks and see the real us—and then to love what you see. That's what we're really looking for, but we're just not sure how to find it.

CHAPTER 2

The Relational Factor

When his dad walked into his room, fifteen-year-old Ken Meyers knew what he would say. It happened like this at least once a week during the school year, sometimes twice.

"I thought you had homework to do," Dad said, lifting the headphones from Ken's ears. Ken bristled inside. He felt like a little kid when his dad just took things away from him like that.

Ken, who had been lying on his bed listening to music, sat up. "I *do* have homework," he said, displaying the language-arts worksheet in his hand, "and I'm doing it." He was halfway through an exercise of diagramming sentences and identifying parts of speech.

"You know you will concentrate better without that noise rattling your brain," Dad insisted, motioning toward the headphones.

"It's not noise, Dad; it's music—*Christian* music." Ken tried to be respectful toward his dad, but he hated these lectures.

Dad's hands went to his hips—his classic lecture pose. "Kenneth, you need to do better on your grades, and to do that you need to concentrate. I was never able to do homework with the TV or radio on. It ruins your concentration."

Ken felt the anger steaming up inside him. *It may ruin* your *concentration, Dad, but it doesn't ruin* mine. *The music actually keeps me relaxed and helps me concentrate. Can't you accept that my study habits may be different from yours?*

"You will have to bear down if you want to achieve the grade level that will get you into State University."

I've tried to tell you that I'm not going to State, Dad, Ken argued silently, biting his lip. *In fact, I don't think I want to go to college right after high school. If you would only listen to me sometimes, you might understand what's going on in my life. But all you can think about are my grades.*

Before Ken could object, his dad picked up the CD player and case of CDs from the bedside table. "Let's put this away until your studies are done, okay?" Then he left the room, closing the door behind him.

Ken was so angry he almost cried. If it wasn't his grades or music Dad and Mom disapproved of, it was his clothes or his hair style or his friends. And when he wanted to show off his latest Christian CD, they were not interested. Ken didn't know which hurt more: their disapproval of him as their son or their passive disinterest in things that interested him. And the fact that his father had taken his music made him feel like a prisoner.

Just before 10:00 P.M., Ken climbed into bed for the night. He had not finished his homework. Tonight's clash with his dad had sapped him of the little motivation he had.

Lying in the darkness, Ken lifted a silent prayer. *God, why are Dad and Mom so against me? Why don't they care about me anymore? I know some things I do really tick them off. But they seem to hate everything about me. It's like they are tired of being my parents and would just rather I would grow up and move out. God, what can I do?*[1]

Ken's experience is representative of the emotional pain experienced by many members of the disconnected generation. It's a common scenario: A teen struggles to find his way through the trying issues that mark this passage in his life. But sometimes the adults he needs most to help him get through it are not there for him. And that only makes the pain worse.

RULES DON'T CONNECT US

When children enter adolescence, sometimes it seems like a metamorphosis gone bad. In some ways, it appears that beautiful butterflies are being transformed into ugly caterpillars. Almost overnight, these cute, cherubic, charming little kids who were a delight to be around suddenly turn into erratic, moody, and unruly teenagers. One minute they are all smiles, and the next minute they blow their stacks or stomp away, sullen and silent. Once-perfect kids can be forgetful, irresponsible, impulsive, contradictory, insolent, and confused—sometimes all in the same day!

A lot of young people, like Ken Meyers, are good kids whose priorities for school, work, money, time management, etc., are all out of whack—or at least they don't match their parents' priorities for them. They are no longer quick to obey or easy to control. In fact, we worry at times if they will soon be totally beyond our control.

So how do adults respond to emerging teenagers? In a generally sincere but misguided attempt to help, many adults, like

Ken's father, think the primary answer to teenage angst and struggle is more structure. So we move in to lay down the law, tighten the reins, and provide needed instruction. We assume that our primary job is to fix the problem, to correct the misbehavior, to enforce the rules, or to right the wrong. But as Ken's story illustrates, well-meaning efforts by parents and other caring adults often leave kids feeling even more alone and disconnected.

"But Josh," parents and church leaders may object, "the Bible lays down clear rules for behavior. We want kids to establish their own identities and to feel connected to us, but they must also learn to obey and to be responsible."

I agree that we must provide clear guidance and hold young people accountable for their actions, even when they feel confused and disconnected. And I believe they need to follow certain rules, even when they think they have the right to make up their own rules. But the critical question is, How do we provide appropriate rules and guidelines for young people without prompting them to disconnect from us relationally and to be captured by the culture?

The answer relates directly to how the rules are presented. For years, I have challenged parents and youth workers to present rules in the context of loving relationships. My deep belief, based on biblical principles, personal research, and my own experience with youth, is that young people do not respond to rules; they respond to relationships. Here are two formulas I often use to illustrate the contrast:

Rules − Relationship = Rebellion
Rules + Relationship = Positive Response

If young people perceive that you are more concerned about the rules than you are about them, they will likely be tempted to disregard your rules. But when they know that they are more important to you than the rules—that you love them no matter what they do or don't do—they are much more likely to follow your guidelines.

Notice how important relationship was to God when He "laid down the law" in the Ten Commandments. Speaking for God, Moses said, "And now, O Israel, what does the LORD your God ask of you but to fear the LORD your God, to walk in all his ways, to love him, to serve the LORD your God with all your heart and with all your soul, and to observe the LORD's commands and decrees that I am giving you today *for your own good*?" (Deut. 10:12–13, emphasis added). As rebellious as Israel was at times, God always treated them like a loving Father, doing everything "for their own good." The Ten Commandments were given to Israel as a safeguard and a blessing, not a burden. The Law was God's loving effort to protect and to provide for His people.

> When they know that they are more important to you than the rules, they are much more likely to follow your guidelines.

Many adults believe that they lay down rules and regulations for their kids "for their own good." But what is often missing is the relational factor. Telling kids "I'm doing this for your own good" will not cut it if they seldom see or hear you demonstrate unconditional love through the time, attention, and care you lavish on them. Rules without relationship lead to a relational disconnect, which prompts rebellion. But rules within a loving relationship usually lead to a positive response.

GRAY MATTER AND INTIMATE CONNECTION

Only recently have I come to understand that *Rules + Relationship = Positive Response* has a significant physiological foundation. With the advent of new technology in neuroscience, brain research has produced startling revelations about the preadult brain. These scientific discoveries shed greater light on the importance of a loving bond between parents and children.

During the last several years, researchers at the National Institute of Mental Health in Bethesda, Maryland, have mapped the brains of nearly one thousand healthy children between the ages of three and eighteen. Their discoveries have virtually dispelled a previously held view that the human brain is fully developed by the time a child reaches puberty. This medical research states:

> Up until the last decade, neuroscientists believed that the billions of neurons in the adolescent brain were as fully matured as the adult brain. But, the neural circuitry or hardware, it turns out, isn't completely installed in most people until their early twenties.[2]

In other words, even when a young person's body has reached maturity, his or her brain has not.

This accounts for the sometimes Jekyll-and-Hyde emotional behavior of most teenagers. A fifteen-year-old boy can be warm and cuddly with his mom one minute and cold as an arctic winter the next. A thirteen-year-old girl may be giggling with her youth minister one minute and yelling angrily at him the next. Medical profession-

> Even when a young person's body has reached maturity, his or her brain has not.

als now believe that these wide adolescent mood swings occur because two different regions of the young person's brain are developing on different timetables.

These two regions are the limbic system, deep in the brain's interior, and the prefrontal cortex, located just behind the forehead. According to today's neuroscientists:

The limbic system is in a stage of high-powered rapid development during adolescence. This is the area of the brain where raw emotions, such as fear and anger, are generated. At the same time, the prefrontal cortex of the brain is on low power and slow development. Decision-making and moral judgments spring from the prefrontal cortex.

The researchers used functional magnetic resonance imaging, a technology that takes a picture of brain activity every three seconds in order to see which parts are being used during processing. Adult brains, the scientists discovered, light up in both the limbic system and the prefrontal cortex when looking at expressions of fright. In teenagers, however, the prefrontal cortex was almost dark while the limbic system lit up.

This is important because the prefrontal cortex acts something like a traffic signal in the brain, keeping tabs on many other parts of the brain, including the limbic system. "The prefrontal cortex," says Karl Pribram, director of the Center for Brain Research and Informational Science at Radford University in Virginia, "is in charge of executive functions." These include the brain's ability to handle ambiguous information and make decisions, to coordinate signals in different regions of the brain, and to tamp down or prolong emotions generated in the limbic system. In an adult, for instance, an overheard insult might arouse a murderous rage, until the prefrontal cortex figures out that the comment was meant for somebody else and tells the limbic system to pipe down. As Pribram puts it, "The prefrontal cortex is the seat of civilization." (See brain diagram.)[3]

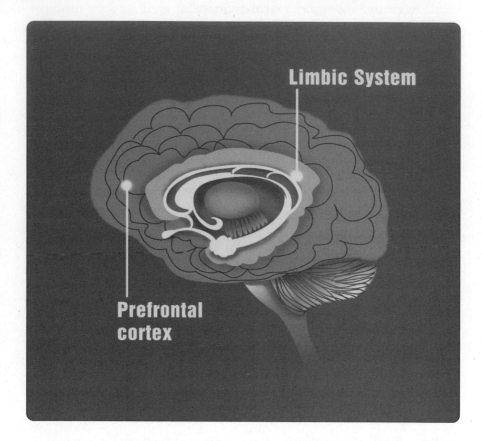

But because the prefrontal cortex in teenagers is not fully mature, it limits to a degree their ability to make sound decisions, especially under the pressure of volatile emotions. The more-developed, highly active limbic system is like a busy highway crowded with speeding cars. The less-developed prefrontal cortex is like a traffic signal that doesn't always work correctly. Sometimes it flashes from green to red without hitting yellow. Sometimes it is green in all directions at the same time, prompting emotional pandemonium. Researchers suspect that this imbalance between the two systems keeps teenagers from tracking multiple concepts and inhibits them from gaining instant access to critical memories and thoughts that are necessary in making sound judgments or controlling unruly emotions.[4]

Imagine your teenagers with limbic systems running at freeway speed, primed to react instantly to anything that might endanger their turf, such as a disagreement with you over fashion, friends, or music. With their prefrontal cortices on overload, teenagers don't always have the brainpower to organize their thoughts and make wise decisions. No wonder our kids often feel confused and disconnected while everything makes perfect sense to us. They aren't fully hard-wired yet!

I'm not implying that young people are little more than flesh-wrapped bundles of neural circuitry devoid of the moral capacity to obey adults and God. They are people, and they must be held responsible for their choices. But by understanding the developmental process of the human brain, we can better understand why kids are prone to wrong choices that seem to make sense to them at the moment. This understanding also better equips us to help them navigate the tough adolescent years.

How Nurture Alters Nature

About three thousand years ago, King Solomon wrote, "Train up a child in the way he should go, even when he is old he will not depart from it" (Prov. 22:6 NASB). Today, modern technology is finally confirming the validity of this scriptural admonition and promise. The way we "train up" our children has even more to do with their behavior than we first thought.

Writing in the publication *Colleagues for Children*, Bruce Perry, M.D., Ph.D., and John Marcellus, M.D., state:

> The brain is very plastic, meaning it is capable of changing in response to experiences, especially repetitive and patterned experiences. Furthermore, the brain is most plastic during early childhood.[5]

According to the article, researchers have discovered that a child's upbringing—the way he or she is "trained up"—actually programs his or her brain. In other words, a child's relational environment has a significant impact on his or her mental development and behavior patterns.

Pioneering research has determined that the brain of a child between the ages of three and eight has twice as many neurons, twice as many connections (synapses), and twice the energy of an adult brain. This lavish overproduction of neural raw material is designed so that the child's brain can adapt to any set of conditions. Also, this overabundance enables the child's mind to flourish despite any physical damage that may occur to the brain. But the research also shows that when children enter adolescence, they undergo a process called "pruning." The *Los Angeles Times* reports:

> As a child grows into a teenager, synapses that are not used are ruthlessly pruned—thousands per second.[6]

Yet, here is the most amazing discovery: Only those synapses that are reinforced by a child's personal experiences are nourished and therefore survive the pruning process. This is because:

The brain develops and modifies itself in response to experience.[7]

In other words, if the emerging teenager is nurtured with an array of positive physical, mental, emotional, and social experiences, that child's brain will develop accordingly. And what happens if he or she is not nurtured?

Neglect [a child] and [his or her] brain connections atrophy almost as quickly as they are formed. Nurturing social relationships are critical. Without them the brain does not grow.[8]

Think about the staggering implications of this discovery! God has given adults the awesome privilege and responsibility of shaping a child's brain by nurturing him or her with positive life experiences. Your young person's very active brain struggles to organize and process thoughts in an attempt to make right choices in life. In the midst of the jumble of thoughts and emotions, he or she naturally feels a little confused and disconnected. Yet you have the opportunity to help clear the confusion and solidify many of those neural connections just by providing a warm, nurturing relationship for your young person. In the process, the decision-making region of his or her brain is allowed greater and easier access to critical memories and emotions.

> Your young person's very active brain struggles to organize and process thoughts in an attempt to make right choices in life.

Here's the bottom line: The better you connect with your young person emotionally and relationally, the better equipped he or she is to sort through the pressures and temptations of life and make right choices. Put another way, rules plus relationship equals positive response.

Think about the conflict between fifteen-year-old Ken Meyers and his dad from the opening pages of this chapter. If Ken had understood how God had designed his brain and responded appropriately, he might have said something like this to his dad's confrontation over listening to CDs and doing homework:

> Dad, I have so many neurons crowding my brain right now that I'm really having trouble following your reasoning. The emotions in my limbic system are overly sensitive, and my underdeveloped prefrontal cortex is confused. As a result, I feel a little disconnected from you right now. I need your instructions, but I also really need you to love me for who I am. That will help me program my neurons with great stuff. As the unused neurons are pruned away, I'll begin to feel better connected to you and God. I'll learn how to make right choices, and my schoolwork will improve. I may even end up going to State University just like you hope.

Fantasy world? Perhaps. But while young people may not be able to verbalize—or even understand—what is going on in their brains, it is clear that they need intimate, loving connections with the significant adults in their world more than they need lectures. God designed that we provide those needed relational connecting points for our young people. It is this nurturing, emotional attachment to you that will equip your kids to deal with the confusion and disconnection they feel.

> They need intimate, loving connections with the significant adults in their world more than they need lectures.

When Kids Are Neglected and Abused

What happens when a child experiences severe neglect and abuse instead of loving nurture from the significant adults in his life? The study by Drs. Perry and Marcellus determined that neglect and abuse adversely influence the development of the young brain, which in turn negatively affects behavior:

> During the traumatic experience, these children's brains are in a state of fear-related activation. This activation of key neural systems in the brain leads to adaptive changes in emotional, behavioral and cognitive functioning to promote survival. Yet, persisting or chronic activation of this adaptive fear response can result in the maladaptive persistence of a fear state. This activation causes hypervigilance, increased muscle tone, a focus on threat-related cues (typically non-verbal), anxiety, behavioral impulsivity—all of which are adaptive during a threatening event yet become maladaptive when the immediate threat has passed.[9]

The studies indicate that children who suffer repeated experiences of abuse, neglect, or terror tend toward impulsive aggression or antisocial personalities. In some, the constant emotional pain of abuse releases an overabundance of stress chemicals that resets the brain's hormone system, placing the child in a "state of fear-related activation." These young people may explode and react, possibly violently, to the threat of danger, but they would usually feel sorrow and remorse afterward.

In other young people, abuse and neglect numb the brain's system of stress hormones. Their ability to feel often dies, and to them nothing hurts. These kids tend to become emotionally insensitive and unresponsive to punishment. These antisocial aggressors feel no remorse for their violent and sometimes murderous acts. I believe this is how the teenagers can coldly pull the trigger and watch their parents and classmates die. Sixteen-year-old Luke Woodham, who killed his mother and then three schoolmates in Pearl, Mississippi, was one such emotionally numbed adolescent. "I killed because people like me are mistreated every day," he stated. "My whole life I felt outcasted, alone."[10]

Obviously, being a mistreated and lonely child is no excuse for killing other human beings. Yet when mistreatment goes undetected and untreated, tragedy is usually not far behind. Your young people may not be impulsive aggressors or antisocial personalities. But it is clear that the treatment young people receive—positive and negative—from the adults in their lives significantly influences their feelings and behavior.

ENTERING THEIR WORLD

Clearly, the relational and emotional experiences of our youth are critical to their development. Rules, regulations, and instructions alone will not foster a relational connection between our kids and us. They need an emotional attachment, a loving bond that only comes as we establish and maintain a deep relationship in our daily interaction with them. Then the rules and instruction we provide will truly be meaningful and fruitful in their lives.

I don't believe God ever intended that we deliver rules or truth to our young people outside a loving, intimate connection with them. As I stated before, we may be able to get our kids to behave well for a while by laying down the law and pressuring them to comply. But unless we also demonstrate our love for them, our youth may not only rebel against our rules, but also disconnect from us relationally. Why? Because God didn't wire kids to respond to rules and regulations. Rather, He wired them to respond to loving relationships in which parents and other caring adults give rules "for their own good" (see Deut. 10:12–13).

So, if we are going to connect relationally with our kids, we must do it up close and personal. We can't instruct from a distance; we must enter their world and relate to them. I'm not talking about trying to live like teenagers—dressing like them, talking like them, listening to their music, and so on. By entering their world, I mean being aware of what's happening in their lives and then being there to make the appropriate relational connection.

> If we are going to connect relationally with our kids, we must do it up close and personal.

What does world of today's youth look like? I see four distinct characteristics.

Emotional Ups and Downs

Someone has said that the world of teenagers is full of hot and cold, nice and nasty. You find them on top of the world one day and struggling under its weight the next. We all experience highs and lows, but adolescents' rises and falls are more frequent and more intense. Many adults tend to minimize these spiking emotional responses because they are often provoked by circumstances that seem trivial to us. But they are not trivial to kids. We must learn to be sensitive to their emotional ups and downs and help them deal with both pleasure and pain.

Conflicts

Young people struggle for individual identity, purpose, and meaning. They are eager to test their wings and see how far they can fly on their own. They want to find out who they are apart from their parents and family. They want a unique identity, but they also want to identify with a group. This is why many students join a club, youth group, team, or gang, even if they must sacrifice personal identity to conform in some way to the group's expectations.

These early experimental flights of independence and identity can create tension and conflict between adults and teenagers. We need to learn how to diffuse the tension and remain relationally connected as our kids seek greater freedom and independence.

Mixed Signals About Love and Sex

The number-one question kids ask me is, "How can I know if I'm really in love?" Many young people, especially preteen and early teen girls, seem to fall in and out of love two or three times a month! These emotional ups and downs level out as they mature, of course, but young people often remain confused about love and sex.

We live in a culture of mixed signals that often distort the biblical concept of love. Many kids grow up mistaking the intensity of sex for the intimacy of love, and this confusion can leave kids emotionally disconnected. If ever they need to feel relationally connected with parents and a caring adult world, it is during this time, when they are learning the difference between true love and what the world often calls love.

Sexual Pressure

Rapid, drastic hormonal changes during adolescence have a profound effect on kids physically, socially, and emotionally. Just as sexual interest and attraction intensify, their ability to make sound judgments is hampered by an overabundance of neural connections. High emotional and hormonal pressure and low self-control are a disastrous combination.

Most of our kids are told what they should and should not do in a relationship with the opposite sex. But knowing the "stop signals" and knowing how and when to observe them are two different things. Young people who feel relationally connected to their parents and other caring adults are substantially less likely to succumb to sexual pressure.

DISCOVERING RELATIONAL CONNECTING POINTS

But if we enter our young people's world to provide the needed guidance and instruction without first connecting with them, we will most likely, as we have said, find resistance. Only a God-ordained relational connection cultivates the heart of a young person and readies him or her to embrace right thinking and right behavior. When young people sense they are secure, significant, lovable, important, authentic, and responsible, they become shaped mentally and emotionally to choose to live in right relationships with you, God, and others.

In Part Two, we will identify six relational connecting points that are designed to equip our young people to make the right moral and relational decisions. In Part Three, we will define and illustrate how to enter our young people's world to make these relational connections. There are issues and obstacles today that make guiding and raising our kids a real challenge. That is why I, along with a team of colleagues, have created more than fifteen resources called the PROJECT 911 family of products. These resources are targeted to help parents, youth workers, Christian educators, parachurch ministers, and pastors to connect to their youth—and to help their youth connect with other youth.

This book acts as the umbrella for the PROJECT 911 family of products. This family includes eight small books in the Friendship 911 collection designed to enable you to know how to help your young person or someone you know who is struggling with such crises as parents' divorce, conflicts with others, the death of a loved one, or past sexual abuse. An entire workbook course with a supplemental video for youth groups takes these eight tough issues and equips kids to know how to respond to each crisis and to their friends who are suffering through the crisis. An adult video course based on this book is also available.

I share this with you because so many parents and youth workers have asked us to provide resources that can help them apply these relational principles to real-life situations. My prayer is that these resources will minister powerfully to you and your young people. (See Appendix A for a complete list of the PROJECT 911 resources.) We need to help our kids navigate through the struggles of adolescence in a less-than-friendly culture. Their survival may depend on it!

A Special Note to Single Parents

If you're a single parent, you may be concerned about how your kids are affected by not having the other parent around (whether physically, emotionally, or both). If possible, share this book with your children's father or mother. Keeping your kids' welfare in mind, you can help your "ex" to be the best possible parent he or she can be. It's in everyone's best interest, and your kids will respect you for it.

If your children's father or mother is no longer around or is not a suitable parent, look for mature, godly people in your church who can provide positive role models as a surrogate father or mother for your kids. Other parents are often delighted to include your kids in family outings or to make special efforts to befriend and talk with your kids.

Raising a child as a single parent is tough. But I believe applying the relational connecting points described in this book will enable you not only to deepen your relationship with your child, but also to discover that God will fill the void of a missing parent.

PART 2

Making the Connection

CHAPTER 3

Connecting Point #1: Affirmation—Giving Youth a Sense of Authenticity

Have you ever heard these stock parental lines? Perhaps they were spoken to you years ago. You may have even made some of the following statements:

- "If you'd listened to me, you wouldn't be in this mess."
- "You have made your bed; now lie in it."
- "Don't come crying to me."
- "There's no point crying over spilled milk."

I suppose these responses were meant to provide some type of instruction following inappropriate behavior. But offering such "wise counsel" to your student will often be met with resistance and will more likely contribute to a relational disconnection between the two of you. The question is, How do we convince our kids that we love them for who they are without approving of their wrong or harmful actions? In short, we follow the example of how God responds to us in such situations.

AFFIRMATION GIVES A SENSE OF AUTHENTICITY

Think for a moment of how Christ went about convincing people to follow Him as "the way and the truth and the life" (John 14:6). Did He simply issue commands left and right in an effort to persuade the masses to forsake their sin and obey God? Was His life consumed only with teaching, preaching, and instructing people on the fine points of God's law?

Brace yourself, because the answer may surprise you. I believe people embraced Christ because of what He taught *and* for who He was. People were drawn not just to His commandments, but also to His compassion to meet the spiritual, emotional, and physical needs of hurting humanity. Now, as then, it is Christ's love that draws us to Him and compels us to believe, to follow, and to obey Him. It is our sense that He understands us and identifies with our wounded hearts and souls that is so irresistible. We deserve punishment, but He validates our need for acceptance. We deserve rejection, but He says we're worth forgiving. We deserve abandonment, but He affirms we're worth saving.

> When young people don't feel that you identify with them, they are less likely to stay connected emotionally to you.

One of the phrases used most often by young people is, "They don't understand me." When young people don't feel that you identify with them, they are less likely to stay connected emotionally to you. And one of the most effective ways to communicate that you identify with them, even when you don't fully understand them, is to affirm their feelings.

Affirm means "to validate or confirm."[1] **When we affirm young people's feelings, we give them a sense of authenticity.** Affirming their feelings tells them that they are real individuals with valid feelings. When we identify with our young people's feelings of excitement or disappointment, we let them know they are understood for who they really are—authentic human beings.

When adolescents blow up in anger, we may be quick to jump all over them with something like, "Get a grip; you're way out of line here!" Or when young people get giddy and noisy over a happy event, we may be less concerned about their joy than we are about them being too loud or too careless in their excitement. But if we move in to affirm their feelings, we confirm that they are real people who are understood.

"Wait a minute, Josh," you may interject. "You can't just let kids vent their feelings all over everybody else. Somebody might get hurt." I agree. I'm talking about *affirming* young people's feelings, not giving them permission to *vent* their feelings any way they like. There's a big difference. Pure emotions are neither right nor wrong. But how a person *expresses* those emotions can be either right or wrong. The apostle Paul reveals this in Ephesians 4:26: "In your anger do not sin." He's not saying it is sinful to be angry; he's warning us not to express our anger in a sinful way. With our kids, it is okay to affirm what they are feeling while at the same time correcting them if they express those feelings in a wrong way.

So how do we affirm young people's feelings so they sense they are understood? How do we emotionally connect with our kids as they tumble through the highs and lows of their emotions? Romans 12:15 is the key: "Rejoice with those who rejoice; mourn with those who mourn." The New Living Translation puts it, "When others are happy, be happy with them. If they are sad, share their sorrow."

While the admonition in Romans 12:15 is profoundly simple, it is not always that easy. You may be tempted to deal with your student's behavior or try to fix his or her problem before affirming his or her feelings. But resist the temptation. Affirm your student's feelings by feeling with him or her before you deal with any resulting behavior. If he is excited over making the team, we need to convey that we are excited with him and for him. If she is disappointed over losing a friend, we must let her know that we are disappointed along with her and for her. If he is upset over a false rumor about him started by a "friend," we need to share how sad we are that he hurts. And when we do, our students will feel like real, authentic people who are being understood—and that will increase the emotional attachment between us and our students.

> Affirm your student's feelings before you deal with any resulting behavior.

Affirming young people's feelings starts with listening to them. The Bible says, "Be quick to listen, slow to speak and slow to become angry" (James 1:19). When we listen to our kids share their activities and feelings, we essentially say to them, "I'm interested in your life's events and how they make you feel." Sit down with your students often and ask, "How are you doing today? What's going on?"—then really listen with interest. Parents, you may find that an excellent time to chat with kids about their thoughts, feelings, and dreams is at dinnertime. Youth workers, chat with your students over a slice of pizza or an ice-cream sundae. Young people are usually more open to conversation during a meal. If you can get them to talk about the day's events, their feelings will probably rise to the surface. Then you can just listen with caring concern and without judgment.

My wife, Dottie, attended a conference once during which the participants were paired up for several minutes to talk about their personal struggles. Dottie's partner poured out her deep hurts, and Dottie listened intently, expressing caring interest. At the end of the time, the woman said, "I cannot express to you how much you have helped me today. I see my problem more clearly. Thanks to you, I have a handle on it now." Dottie had hardly said a word! For the most part, she had just listened. You will be amazed at how listening attentively and with a compassionate heart will help your kids feel that they are understood and validated as people.

A second key to affirming young people's feelings is to respond actively. When they are up, we must respond by rejoicing with them. When they are down, we must mourn with them. Let's talk about each separately.

When the Emotional Elevator Is on the Top Floor

As I write this book, our eldest daughter, Kelly, is in her first year of medical school. Recently she agonized over a tough exam she had taken, dreading that her score might not meet her expectations. Later, she called, excited to tell me she had passed with a very good score. She was thrilled, and so was I. I said something like, "Great going, Kelly! I am so thrilled for you." Then I sent her a bouquet of flowers to further express my excitement.

It has taken me a while to learn the important connecting skill of rejoicing with my kids over their triumphs. I used to be quick to "mourn" and slow to "rejoice." Are you the same way? Is all your emotional energy spent on picking up the pieces after a blowup or a breakdown in your young person's life? When he or she is doing well, are you just glad not to be in his or her face? Maybe that's why

Paul first mentioned rejoicing in Romans 12:15. We need to be just as affirming and involved during our kids' ups as we are during their downs, even for minor joys and blessings in their lives. This is one of the ways our heavenly Father bonds with us. The prophet Zephaniah wrote, "The LORD your God is with you, he is mighty to save. He will take great delight in you, he will quiet you with his love, he will rejoice over you with singing" (Zeph. 3:17). Rejoicing with our kids is an important way to build a strong emotional attachment to them.

How do you affirm young people's feelings of joy and excitement? You can do it through what you say. Lavish them with comments like, "I'm so happy for you!"; "This is so great!"; "I'm so excited that this happened to you!"; "You have every right to be thrilled; I am too!"; etc. You can also affirm their feelings through what you do. Rejoicing times sometimes call

> Rejoicing with our kids is an important way to build a strong emotional attachment to them.

for celebrations and gifts, but they don't have to be extravagant. Take your young person out for lunch, dinner, or ice cream; buy him or her a new CD; allow a special privilege; or send an encouraging card. You may not be as excited as your kids are, but if you mirror their joys by rejoicing with them, they will feel validated, and you will solidify the loving bond between you.

WHEN THE EMOTIONAL ELEVATOR IS IN THE BASEMENT

Arriving home from an evening out, your seventeen-year-old son confesses that he got into a fender bender with the family car. How will you respond?

Your fourteen-year-old daughter, a B-plus student, brings home a report card with three Cs and a D. What will you say to her?

An athletic high-school girl in your youth group calls in tears, saying she has been cut from the volleyball team by a coach who doesn't like her. What will your first words be?

A freshman boy comes to a youth event with abrasions on his face, admitting that he got into a fight with another boy. How will you handle it?

These trying situations, and countless others like them, reflect life as usual in the activity of raising and ministering to adolescents. Kids make mistakes. Kids have problems. Kids get hurt. Kids get into trouble. Kids are victimized by other kids—and even by adults. Sometimes these incidents are genuine crises: a life-threatening disease or injury, the breakup of a serious relationship, the death of a friend or relative, an unplanned pregnancy, etc. But most of the time, they are the relatively minor disappointments, losses, conflicts, and hurts of everyday life. Dealing with difficulties goes with the territory of raising and ministering to young people.

The critical question is, How do you deal with kids in the day-to-day difficulties of life? If your first response is to enforce the rules, to correct the behavior, or to fix the problem, you may be prodding your youth toward a relational disconnection that will cause him or her to rebel against you and the truth you wish to impart. But if your rule enforcement, behavior correction, and problem fixing are preceded by and enveloped in loving care and concern through which you identify with his or her feelings, you increase the opportunity to strengthen your relational connection with young people. And the stronger the connection between adult and youth, the more likely they will be to willingly receive your direction, correction, or advice.

CONNECTING THE WAY GOD CONNECTS WITH US

How does God want us to respond to young people when they are disappointed or hurting? The same way He responds to our disappointments and hurts. He mourns with us and lovingly comforts us. God touches me with His love in a number of ways during my down times. Two Scripture passages have been especially encouraging to me over the years. Jeremiah 31:3 reads, "I have loved you with an everlasting love; I have drawn you with loving-kindness." The apostle John wrote, "This is love: not that we loved God, but that he loved us and sent his Son as an atoning sacrifice for our sins" (1 John 4:10). Knowing that God loves me no matter how sad I feel or how I may have failed comforts me.

I often think of a line from the old Gaither song, "I Am Loved": "The one who knows me best loves me most."[2] Being assured that God loves me right where I am really ministers to me. I am also blessed to realize that the ones who know me next-to-most—Dottie, our four great kids, and my longtime friend Dick Day—love me next-to-most. God often communicates His compassion, concern, and comfort to me through my family, my friend Dick, and others. And God wants to use you as a channel of His comfort and love in your kids' lives.

> God wants to use you as a channel of His comfort and love in your kids' lives.

We get a beautiful picture of God's compassion and concern in the parable of the good Samaritan (see Luke 10:30–37). The priest and the Levite avoided getting involved with the man who was beaten and left for dead. But the Samaritan saw a man in deep distress and ministered to his need. The good

Samaritan didn't stop to ask, "Was this your fault? Did you deserve this beating? Should you have been more careful on your journey?" Instead, he felt compassion for the man and did what he could to relieve the man's suffering. Jesus concluded the story by saying, "Go and do likewise" (v. 37). We are to reach out to our hurting kids and to heal their hurts, regardless of how they got them.

How do you think God feels when you or your kids are hurt or discouraged? I believe Scripture reveals that He hurts for us all—yet without even a taint of our sin. In John 11, Jesus was touched to the point of tears by Mary and Martha's grief over the death of their brother and Jesus' friend, Lazarus. I believe that the daily disappointments and hurts in our lives and our young people's lives—whether they are relatively minor, such as unkind words, or major, such as the wrenching pain of the death of a loved one—touch God's heart with sorrow and pain. What if the pain is our own fault, the consequence of ignoring God's protection and provision by violating His law? Pain is pain, and their pain touches God's heart. Remember, He separates who we are from what we do, even when what we do is wrong.

During the time before the Flood, "the LORD saw how great man's wickedness on the earth had become, and that every inclination of the thoughts of his heart was only evil all the time" (Gen. 6:5). Consider the depth of the darkness reflected in these words: *Every* inclination was *only* evil *all* the time. And how did God feel about the sin that drove His human creation to destruction? We may be tempted to project on Him some of the responses we feel when our young people disobey us and must pay the price: "I told you not to do it, but you wouldn't listen"; "It serves you right for disobeying me"; "I don't feel sorry for you one bit, because you brought this on yourself." If anyone had reason to vent righteous indignation and an "I-told-you-so" attitude, God did.

But is this how God felt about His fallen creatures in Genesis? Look at the next verse: "The LORD was grieved that he had made man on the earth, and his heart was filled with pain" (v. 6). In His righteousness and truth, God had to judge sin with the Flood. But His heart was "filled with pain" for His human creation over what sin had done to them. It doesn't matter whether the source of pain is our own sin, someone else's sin, or just the unfortunate circumstances of life. God is touched with our hurt, and He comforts us at the connecting point of our pain. We need to respond in the same way when our kids are emotionally down.

How does God respond to our hurts? One of His responses is to provide comfort. Jesus taught, "Blessed are those who mourn, for they will be comforted" (Matt. 5:4). Where does this comfort come from? It comes from "the God and Father of our Lord Jesus Christ, the Father of compassion and the God of all comfort, who comforts us in all our troubles" (2 Cor. 1:3–4). Paul identifies God so closely with the comfort we all need that he calls Him the "God of all comfort." God provides His comfort directly from Himself and through the ministry of others who have likewise received His comfort.

The God who hurts when we hurt compassionately surrounds us with the comfort we need. God's comfort is just one way He reaches out to connect with us in loving relationship. Similarly, our concern and comfort when our young people are emotionally low are vital to maintaining an intimate connection with them.

Affirming my children's feelings through rejoicing and comforting hasn't come naturally to me. You will learn through the course of this book that I came from a home with an alcoholic father, and I didn't have many positive parenting role models. So I have reached out for every bit of help I could get. I've read all the parenting books I could get my hands on, studied the lives of people who seem to have it together, and taken in all the advice and counsel from wise, experienced laypersons and professionals. One person who has impacted my life personally and contributed greatly to the Project 911 resources is David Ferguson of Intimate Life Ministries in Austin, Texas. Many of the insights in these resources are derived from the biblical principles and teachings of David Ferguson. (See Appendix B for more information about Intimate Life Ministries.)

PROVIDING A COMFORT ZONE

When a young child falls down and scrapes his knee, what does he do first? He runs crying to Mom or Dad. And what does the parent do? He or she holds the child and pats him tenderly while offering soothing words like, "Oh, you fell down. I'm so sorry your knee got hurt. Let me hold you until it feels better." Even if their wounds are minor, little kids seem to deeply crave the comforting touch and words of a caring adult.

In reality, kids—and adults, for that matter—never outgrow the need to be comforted when they experience physical, emotional, or relational pain. Young people no longer climb up in our laps when they feel sad, nor do they ask us to kiss their "owies" when they are hurt. Yet their greatest need in the face of life's difficulties, troubles, and pain is often to receive comfort. One major way God shares His comfort

> Kids—and adults, for that matter—never outgrow the need to be comforted when they experience physical, emotional, or relational pain.

with us is through other people. The apostle Paul wrote, "God . . . comforts us in all our troubles, so that we can comfort those in any trouble with the comfort we ourselves have received from God" (2 Cor. 1:3–4). Due to your critical role in a young person's life as a parent or youth leader, the comfort you provide when he or she is feeling down is vital to how well he or she connects with you and receives needed instruction or correction.

What is comfort? Perhaps it will help to understand first what comfort is *not*.

Comfort is not a pep talk urging the student to hang in there, tough it out, or hold it together.

Pep talks convey the hope that "God is in control" and "everything is going to be all right." This may give hope for the future, but it gives little comfort for the young person's present pain.

Comfort is not an attempt to explain why bad things happen to people.

A lecture on cause and effect, deeds and consequences, or even God's perfect and permissive will may provide helpful insight at some point, but it rarely gives comfort in the moment of pain, sorrow, and discouragement.

People receive comfort primarily when someone feels their hurt and sorrow with them. Earlier, we mentioned Jesus' ministry of comfort when His friend Lazarus died (see John 11). When Jesus arrived at the home of Lazarus's sisters, Mary and Martha, He wept with them (see vv. 33–35). His response is especially interesting in light of what He did next: He raised Lazarus from the dead (see vv. 38–44).

Why didn't Jesus simply tell the grieving Mary and Martha, "No need to cry, My friends; in a few minutes Lazarus will be alive again"? Because at that moment they were hurting and just needed someone to cry with them. Jesus connected with their deep need for comfort by sharing in their sorrow and tears. Later He performed the miracle that turned their sorrow into joy.

Young people are comforted in their difficulties when they know that someone else understands their hurt. Whenever a student is upset over a disappointing or hurtful experience, he is "mourning." According to God's design, stated in Romans 12:15, you connect with him at that point by affirming his feelings and by mourning with him. In other words, put yourself in his shoes, try to sense what he is feeling, and respond accordingly. The result is comfort.

For example, sixteen-year-old Jessica comes up to you with a cloud of gloom hanging over her. "I lost my job," she says dejectedly. You may be tempted to respond in a number of different ways: "How did it happen? Did you mess up and get fired?"; "Cheer up, you'll find another job"; "The Bible says all things work together for good, so hang in there." These responses may address Jessica's *problem,* but they don't address her *pain.* She is hurting emotionally, and she needs someone to mourn with her so she can be comforted. Once you comfort her, you can consider other ways of helping her deal with the issue at hand.

You comfort Jessica by first assessing how she feels. She has just lost her job, so she likely feels rejected, even if she was fired because of her own mistakes. Have you experienced a similar disappointment? She may feel angry or bitter toward her former employer, sad that her source of spending money has been cut off, or fearful that she won't find another job. Can you identify with how she feels? Then you are ready to be God's channel of comfort to Jessica.

In Jessica's situation, comfort may sound something like this: "Jessica, I'm so sorry you lost your job. I know you feel awful about it, and I feel sad for you. It hurts me to see you hurt so." Sincere, heartfelt words like this, sometimes accompanied by a gentle hug or pat, will help Jessica sense that your care for her and how she feels supersedes your questions about what happened.

A friend's experience with comfort taught me an important lesson I want to share with you. Once, when his wife was at a very low point emotionally, my friend, in an effort to comfort her, said, "Honey, I know just what you're going through." She snapped back angrily, "No you don't! How dare you say you know what I'm going through." My friend was speechless, but his wife was right. "Mourn with those who mourn" does not mean that we *experience* someone's pain, because we can't necessarily participate in his or her unique experience. Rather, it means we *hurt* with that person because the experience hurt him or her. My friend should have said, "Honey, what you're going through must be tough, and I want you to know that I care and hurt for you."

That's how we affirm young people's sorrow and pain without giving the impression that we know exactly how they feel—which they know is not true. You might consider using words similar to these when you comfort a young person: "What you're going through must really hurt you, and I want to let you know that I hurt for you." You will be amazed and pleased at how your timely words and gestures of comfort will help strengthen the connecting bond between you and your kids.

DEAL WITH FEELINGS BEFORE ISSUES

When our son, Sean, was in high school, he played basketball for a coach who loved the kids and wanted them to win but ran the team by intimidation and degradation. He yelled at the boys and berated them when they played poorly or made mistakes. Sean didn't like it, but he wanted to play basketball so badly that he hung in there.

During one of the games I attended, the coach got after Sean in a big way. The way he yelled at Sean was awful. I could tell that Sean was especially hurt by the coach's cruel tactics, and I hurt for him. When he came home, I said, "You were hurt by the way Coach got after you today, right?" He nodded dejectedly. I continued, "That must have hurt so badly when the coach said those things. Sean, nobody works harder to be a good basketball player than you do. I truly hurt for you." We really connected over the incident, and he seemed to be helped by my comfort.

Later that week, I asked Sean's permission to talk to the school administration about the hard-handed tactics of the coach. "You would do that?" he responded, amazed. I said I would if he agreed, and he did. I made an appointment with the school superintendent and athletic director, and I confronted the coach in front of them about how he was demoralizing Sean and the other members of the team. The school dealt with the issue, and the problem was completely resolved. Sean was deeply touched that I affirmed his feelings and then came to his defense and dealt with the troubling issue.

Behind your student's feelings of anger, disappointment, and hurt is usually an issue that must be addressed. The hurt and the source of the hurt must be separated in your thinking and addressed differently. A key to developing a loving bond with your young person is to deal with feelings before you deal with issues. In Sean's case, I had to deal with his wounded spirit before I dealt with the school administration over the offensive tactics of the coach.

Too often we jump on the issue before dealing with the feelings of hurt it caused. We must comfort the hurt before correcting the problem. For example, one time Dottie came home from a meeting at school very hurt over what some other mothers had said about one of our kids. When this happened before, I often would leap to her defense by saying something like, "Honey, don't let it get to you. Here's what you need to do." Then I would outline a plan to fix the problem. It may have been a good plan, but it didn't address the pain Dottie felt. So on this particular occasion, I simply put my arms around her and said, "Honey, I'm so sorry that you had to hear those words, and I hurt for you." That was it, no fix-it plan. A couple of days later, after the bad feelings had subsided, Dottie brought up the issue, and we were able to discuss it and come up with a plan of action.

> Behind your student's feelings of anger, disappointment, and hurt is usually an issue that must be addressed.

Address your students' feelings first by supplying the affirmation and comfort they need. Then, when it is appropriate, address the problem. When you affirm your students' feelings, they gain a sense of authenticity, which provides an open door to a deeper relational connection.

Affirming young people's feelings by rejoicing with them and mourning with them is just the first of six vital relational connecting points. You also need to connect by accepting them for who they are—apart from what they do.

CHAPTER 4

Connecting Point #2: Acceptance—Giving Youth a Sense of Security

Katie was warming up for one of her most important games of the season. She ran off the field and came over to me. "Daddy," she asked with excitement, "if I score a goal, will you give me a dollar?"

"Sure," I answered with a smile.

"Wow!" Katie said. To a six-year-old, one dollar for each goal sounded like a professional sports contract.

"Wait a minute," I said, grabbing her before she ran off to join her team. "Even if you don't score a goal, I'll still give you a dollar."

"You will?"

"Yes, I will."

"Wow!" Katie said again as she prepared to scamper off to start the game.

But I grabbed her one more time, asking, "Do you know why?"

For at least three years, I had been trying to help Katie understand what acceptance was all about, and none of it had seemed to mean much to her. But at that moment, she looked at me and said, "Yeah, it doesn't matter if I play soccer or not. You love me anyway!"

My daughter couldn't have said anything at the moment to give me more joy. I don't even remember if she scored a goal that day. It didn't matter. What did matter was that she knew that I loved her anyway. That's what acceptance is all about.

When we accept young people for who they are, we give them a sense of security. Acceptance deals with embracing people for who they are, rather than for what they do. When your young people feel accepted by you, they are more likely to be vulnerable and transparent, opening up greater trust between you. Feeling accepted for just being themselves creates a secure feeling that no matter what happens, they'll be loved. That kind of accepting relationship creates a loving bond and an intimate relational connection between you and your students.

Accepting Our Kids As We Have Been Accepted

Paul exhorts us, "Accept one another, then, just as Christ accepted you" (Rom. 15:7). How does Christ accept us? Unconditionally, right where we are, warts and all. He doesn't wait until we are living in the truth before inviting us into relationship with Him; He invites us into a relationship with Him while we are yet sinners so that He might lead us into living the truth.

The Gospels give us a clear picture of God's acceptance as expressed through the life of His Son. For example, the Samaritan woman in John 4 had three strikes against her socially: She was a woman, inferior to men in that culture; she was a Samaritan, despised by the Jews; and she was immoral, living with a man who was not her husband. Though He did not condone her sin, Jesus engaged her in conversation without judgment or condemnation. As a result, the woman welcomed the truth when Jesus shared it, and her life was changed.

In John 8, Christ was summoned to judge a woman caught in the act of adultery. When He refused to condone the vindictive plot of the religious leaders, He was left alone with the woman. Listen to the acceptance in His words, followed by a precept intended to protect and provide for the woman: "Neither do I condemn you. . . . Go now and leave your life of sin" (v. 11).

The Pharisees of His day criticized Jesus for fraternizing with "tax collectors and 'sinners'" (Matt. 9:11). Jesus replied, "It is not the healthy who need a doctor, but the sick" (v. 12). How does a doctor respond to a person who comes to him with an illness or injury? Does the doctor condemn the poor patient for being sick? Does he say something like, "How stupid of you. If you had been paying better attention, you would not have hit your thumb with the hammer"? Of course not! The physician accepts the patient right where he or she is and focuses on providing the comfort and healing he or she needs.

> If we are to strengthen the loving bond with our young people, we, too, must accept them for who they are, no matter what.

This is how God connects with us when we are in pain, trouble, or crisis. He doesn't condemn us or criticize us, even though we may be in the wrong. God does not condone or overlook our sin; it must be dealt with on His terms. But He loves us for who we are and accepts us at the point of our failure. Remember, Christ died for us so that God might forgive us and form a personal and eternal relationship with us. And if we are to strengthen the loving bond with our young people, we, too, must accept them for who they are, no matter what.

CONNECTING WITH YOUNG PEOPLE THROUGH LOVING ACCEPTANCE

When young people sense genuine acceptance from the significant adults in their lives, they feel connected and secure. They need to know that their value to you is not determined by how well they perform or whether they fail to perform. This is never more true than when young people are hurting or in trouble. They need to feel that you accept them and love them for who they are, even when you do not approve of their actions.

Most adults will agree that "acceptance, period" is the ideal they aim for with their kids, and many believe they are hitting the target. In reality, however, the acceptance they offer is often conditional. As long as students are following the rules, staying out of trouble, and doing what is expected of them, they may find their parents and significant adults to be accepting and agreeable. But when young people make a mistake, break a rule, or act bratty or unreasonable, they sometimes can be made to feel

> Acceptance is a full-time job.

like second-class citizens. Adults sometimes talk to them differently, become cool and distant, or withhold affection. Adults can withdraw their acceptance very subtly, without even realizing it. But kids sense the change instantly.

Acceptance is a full-time job. You don't vow to be an accepting adult around young people and then assume that communicating acceptance is automatically part of your nature. Take every opportunity to let your kids know they are totally accepted by you, whether they win or lose life's daily battles and challenges. They are human, just like you; they have good days and days that are not so good. But commit to making sure they sense your acceptance every day.

Most young people find a particular time of the year most depressing: the day they get their report cards. Why? Most parents don't separate performance from acceptance. When your children get good grades, say something like: "I so appreciate the hard work you put in to make those As. But honey, I don't love you because you're a good student. If you never got an A in your life, I would love you just as much." What you are trying to do is separate what they do from who they are.

Youth leaders can also fall into the trap of conditional acceptance. Make every effort to communicate to your students that you accept them for who they are, not for what they do. Students who forgot their Bible study homework or missed a leadership meeting or lost their permission slip for youth camp need to know that you still care about them, even when they mess up.

Your son or daughter is always your son or daughter, a gift from God and worthy of your love and acceptance. The kids in your youth group are always individuals for whom Christ died, worthy of your love and acceptance. Totally accepting kids doesn't mean that we approve of everything they do. But we must go to great lengths to let them know we accept them for who they are, then we can deal separately with their behavior as necessary.

Remember, acceptance is based on who a person is—a human being made in God's image with infinite value, dignity, and worth. Kids treated with complete acceptance stand a much better chance of viewing themselves as persons of worth. And when they sense they are valued for who they are, they are much more likely to feel secure in their relationships with parents and other adults.

What does acceptance sound like? Accepting words focus more on a person's value and worth than on his or her performance. Here are some phrases you can use to communicate that you not only appreciate what your kids do, but you also accept them for who they are:

- "You are so wonderfully creative."
- "You have a great sense of humor."
- "You have such a caring heart."
- "I love your enthusiasm."

When we focus on such qualities as diligence, dependability, creativity, courage, persistence, and patience in our young people, we communicate that we love them for who they are, not just for what they do.

On the other hand, conditional acceptance focuses on performance. This is when acceptance is only given when a person obeys, achieves, or performs well. So when their performance is not up to certain standards, young people can naturally feel rejected. And such rejection can lead to a loss of worth and value as a person. A willingness to be vulnerable and transparent can fade along with trust between youth and adult.

All people—especially young people—want to be accepted. If kids don't sense acceptance from the adults they love and trust most, they will find some way to get it, even if what they do is very unacceptable to those around them. Why is this true? I believe the answer relates to how God created us and relates to us. We put such importance on acceptance because it seems to be God's first building block in developing human beings. God, the heavenly Father, does want to see the behavior of His children changed. But before He endeavors to change us, He first meets us right where we are—through grace. The more firmly we grasp this principle, the more intimately we can bond with young people. We must accept kids where they are—apart from their behavior. This is what makes kids feel secure in relationships. And if they don't feel secure in their relationship with us, our efforts to change their behavior will be largely unproductive.

> We must accept kids where they are—apart from their behavior.

ACCEPTANCE PROMOTES A HEALTHY VIEW OF SELF

In my travels, I am constantly meeting young people who have known only conditional acceptance or very little acceptance at all.

Mark knows he can never get to college because when he was younger, a teacher constantly told him he was stupid. Worse yet, his parents repeatedly told him, "You're lazy, and you'll never amount to anything."

Lori grew up with her friends teasing her unmercifully about her skinny legs. They taunted her by calling her "Bird Legs" and saying, "You'd better wear skis in the shower so you don't slip down the drain." Later, as a junior in college, Lori was slender while many of her classmates battled weight problems. Yet she still apologized for her skinny legs and avoided being seen in public in a swimsuit.

Jeff comes across as self-assured and confident. He's at the top of his class and plays first-string football. Jeff's philosophy is, "You've got to produce; otherwise nobody thinks you're worth much."

In some people like Mark and Lori, a poor sense of self-worth is easy to spot because they openly admit their insecurities and negative opinions of themselves. Others, like Jeff, try to hide their low view of themselves with a brash, aggressive attitude. Deep down, however, they are also insecure and unsure.

"Unsure of what?" you may ask. Unsure that they are accepted, that they have worth and real value in themselves apart from what they do. Instead, these students live on a performance basis, believing that they have to prove to others and to themselves that they are worthy of being loved and accepted.

Sadly, many young people have fallen into the performance trap, along with their parents and other adult role models. They fail to understand that God's unconditional love gives every human being worth. As the psalmist wrote, "What is man that you are mindful of him, the son of man that you care for him? You made him a little lower than the heavenly beings and crowned him with glory and honor" (Ps. 8:4–5).

Ironically, I frequently meet people who doubt that it is biblical to view ourselves as persons of value and worth. After speaking to adults, I am often challenged by someone who is disturbed that I talk about our self-worth. They contend that the concept of self-worth focuses attention on self instead of God. Whenever I am challenged this way, I usually respond by saying something like this: "I appreciate your willingness to talk about this. While I agree that people can become self-centered and all wrapped up in self-interests, I don't agree that self-worth is a sinful idea. In fact, I believe that a proper understanding of our worth and value as God's creation is exactly what keeps us from becoming selfish and self-centered. The apostle Paul encouraged 'every man among you not to think more highly of himself than he ought to think; but to think so as to have sound judgment, as God has allotted to each a measure of faith' [Rom. 12:3 NASB]."

Paul is not saying in this verse that we should not think highly of ourselves. He is saying that we should not think more highly of ourselves than *what we really are*. In other words, we should be realistic and biblical in our opinions of ourselves. That's why Paul added that we are "to think so as to have sound judgment."

> He says that we should not think more highly of ourselves than what we really are.

The verb *to think* in the Greek means "to think or to feel a certain way about a person." In Romans 12:3, it refers to "forming an opinion, a judgment, or a feeling about yourself."[1] Paul's point is that we should form this opinion or self-concept as a result of a realistic appraisal of ourselves.

Susan is a young career woman whose former job required her to be around other attractive women daily. She is very good-looking by contemporary standards, but she does not see herself that way. Since Susan's teenage years, her mother has repeatedly told Susan that she is not shaped right. Instead of recognizing her value and worth as God's creation, Susan identifies herself as ugly and inadequate. She is convinced that no man will ever like her because her figure is imperfect. In her job, the more she saw women she considered beautiful, the worse Susan began to feel about herself. Her insecurity over her appearance began to affect the quality of her work, and she eventually lost her job.

Sam was disfigured, the result of a childhood accident that left his face permanently scarred. As a teenager, he suffered rejection from his peers, particularly from girls. His distorted sense of identity could be summarized in one word: *freak*. As a result, Sam withdrew socially and escaped into an unreal world, spending up to twenty hours each week watching movies. Sam considered the darkness of the movie theater an appropriate place for the freak he considered himself to be.

Even if your young person is regarded as a nobody at home, school, or church, he or she is somebody to God. Whether any of us are ever perceived as beautiful or accomplished, our infinite worth and value to God are undiminished. A healthy self-worth really comes down to *seeing yourself as God sees you—no more and no less.*

> A healthy self-worth really comes down to seeing yourself as God sees you—no more and no less.

Whenever I get into a discussion on self-worth, I usually recommend the book *Seeing Yourself as God Sees You*.[2] It may also help you gain a clearer biblical view of your worth in God's eyes, as well as the worth of your young people.

Students with a healthy, biblical sense of self-worth can accept themselves as God accepts them because they know God delights in them. This acceptance is not based on anything we have done, but rather on the fact that God created us in His image and sent His Son to die on the cross for us. Biblical self-worth believes, "I am lovable, and I am a capable and competent part of God's creation. I know I'm not perfect, but I have been redeemed by God.

He has forgiven me for my sins, and I can become all He wants me to be."

You can see why young people with a healthy sense of self-worth feel more secure. They believe that they matter, that the world is a better place because they are here. Students with a healthy self-view are better prepared to interact and to connect with parents and other adults, appreciating their worth as well. These kids radiate hope, joy, and trust.

In contrast, students with a poor sense of their worth to God and to others are slaves to the opinions of their peers and the adults in their lives. Unable to see themselves as God sees them, they are not free to be themselves, and conflicts and disconnection from others often result.

THE REAL MEANING OF PROVERBS 22:6

Our young people need to know that they are accepted as unique individuals. One of the best descriptions of a child's uniqueness is found in the familiar words penned by King Solomon: "Train up a child in the way he should go, even when he is old he will not depart from it" (Prov. 22:6 NASB). Unfortunately, this verse is often misunderstood—and misapplied—by those who are responsible for the training of young people. Many parents and youth leaders think it means "Have family devotions, make sure kids attend Sunday school and youth group, and when they are grown up, they will not depart from the faith."

The real meaning of this verse, however, centers on the phrase "the way he should go." The writer is referring to the *child's* way, not God's. The root meanings of these words suggest stimulating a desire for guidance according to each child's own uniqueness.

In Psalms, the same Hebrew word is translated "bend" and refers to the bending of the archer's bow (see Pss. 11:2; 64:3). Today, with precision manufacturing, almost anyone can pick up a forty-five-pound bow and do a great job of hitting the target. But in biblical days, nothing was standardized. Every archer made his own bow and had to know the unique characteristics of that bow if he hoped to hit anything with it.

In the same way, adults need to know the unique characteristics of each young person in their lives. Training up each one in "the way he should go" doesn't mean you let him run wild or allow him to get his own way all the time. In the *Ryrie Study Bible,* a note for Proverbs 22:6 explains that "'the way he should go' really means 'according to his way; i.e., the child's habits and interests. The instruction must take into account his individuality and inclinations, his personality, the unique way God created him, and must be in keeping with his physical and mental development.'"[3]

Just as the archer would find the particular bend of his bow, you must find the particular bend of each of your young people. Parents know instinctively that each of their kids is different, but they still often make the mistake of training and disciplining each one in essentially the same way. Perhaps this comes from having the same expectations for all of them. I agree that families need standards by which to operate, but there is no standard way to treat all kids because each kid responds differently to how he or she is treated. In fact, "standardized" training and discipline is one of the best ways to disconnect from your young people.

As a youth worker, you may find that different kids respond in different ways to you. Take, for example, your attempt to settle down a rowdy youth-group meeting. Some will quiet right down by a gentle, "Okay, let's settle down now." Others seem as if they need a hammerlock to get them quiet. I know that as a parent, I can't discipline my daughter, Heather, in the same way I disciplined my son, Sean. Why? God created each of them uniquely. And unless we understand the "bend" in the "bows" God has entrusted to us, we are apt to "miss the target," so to speak.

As we stated in chapter 2, medical science is discovering that each child's brain is like plastic, ready to be shaped by his or her environment. No two brains are exactly alike, so each child must be nurtured and disciplined according to his or her uniqueness. To affirm a young person's uniqueness and accept his or her specialness, constantly remind him or her, "If there is no one else like you, why not be the 'unique you' that God created in the first place? You are the best *you* there will ever be!" This is one of the best ways I know to convey acceptance and to nurture a loving bond between an adult and a young person.

> Each child must be nurtured and disciplined according to his or her uniqueness.

ACCEPTING NO MATTER WHAT

My daughter Kelly and I have a great relationship. We have really sensed a deep relational connection over the years, and our conflicts have been minor and short-lived. I believe a significant contributor to our closeness has been my effort to convey acceptance to her. For example, when Kelly was thirteen, she gave me a golden opportunity to tell her that I accept her for who she is, not for what she does or doesn't do.

I picked her up one day after school and decided to meet her at the door as she came out. As we walked across the parking lot to the car, out of the blue she brought up the name of a well-known Christian leader—I'll call him Jack Smith—who had fallen into immorality. Kelly asked, "Daddy, what do you think of Jack Smith?"

Jack Smith had been all over the news, but I had no idea that he had become discussion material for a secular junior high classroom. Whenever I get a tough question from my kids, I often answer their question with a question of my own. This gives me a context that helps my thinking. (It also helps me to buy time to think of the right answer!)

"Why do you ask?" I responded.

"Oh, in class today we spent an entire hour talking about Reverend Smith and everything he did with that other woman. I just wondered what you thought about what he did."

All kinds of responses flashed through my mind. I thought about what most adults might say: "Oh, I think that's awful. I think it's disgusting. They ought to throw him out of the ministry. He's probably not even a real Christian!"

I had been hearing pastors say this kind of thing to their congregations, and while I understood their outrage, I also realized something else. Any pastor saying things like that about Jack Smith was only succeeding in telling the young people in his church: "If you ever get into trouble, don't come to me as your pastor." In particular, he was sending this message to all students in his congregation: "As your pastor, I'll love and accept you if you stay pure. But if you get involved in premarital sex, I'll condemn you."

Christian parents who spoke about Jack Smith in negative, judgmental terms were only managing to communicate this message to their own kids: "We only love and accept you if you don't get on drugs, if you don't drink, if you don't get pregnant, if you don't listen to bad music, if you don't color your hair green . . . ," etc.

So how should I answer Kelly? How could I walk the line between telling her what I thought of Jack Smith's sin while also communicating that I still "loved" Jack Smith? I swallowed hard, bit my lip, and said, "Honey, what Jack Smith did was wrong. It was sin." I took time to explain to Kelly why it was sin. Then I quickly went on. "But, Kelly, you need to realize something. Your teacher and all the kids in your class need to realize that God loves Jack Smith as much as He loves you and me. Everyone needs to realize that Christ died for Jack Smith as much as He died for you and me. If God can't forgive Jack Smith, then He can't forgive you and me."

As we continued walking across the parking lot toward the car, Kelly said nothing for a few moments. I tried to think of how to put into words what I really wanted her to know: *I don't love you because you're a virgin. If you ever get pregnant, you can come to your dad because, just as I want to minister the grace of God to Jack Smith, I want to minister the grace of God to you, my daughter.*

Taking a deep breath, I stopped Kelly, turned her to face me, and said, "Honey, let's look at this realistically. If you got pregnant, can you imagine what your dad would go through because of my message on sexual purity? Half the people here in our own church would turn on me."

Kelly looked up at me, her brown eyes wide with concern, and said, "I know that, Dad."

"But I want you to know one thing," I continued. "If you ever did get pregnant, I wouldn't care what all these people would say.

I'd turn my back on all of them, but I'd never turn my back on you. I'd put my arms around you, and we would see it through together."

At that moment, my thirteen-year-old daughter dropped her books on the pavement and started crying. She threw her arms around me and exclaimed, "I know you would, Daddy!"

"Well," I said with a chuckle, "I'm just going to keep reminding you." To myself, I thought, *And I'm going to keep reminding myself what I said today.*

That encounter happened several years ago. Since then, I have made it a point to remind Kelly on various occasions that I accept her, that I trust her, and that I love her no matter what might happen. Some people might think I'm taking too big a risk, that perhaps Kelly might "take me up on my offer." Or she might get careless, thinking, *It doesn't matter, because Dad will love me anyway.* But I don't worry about that, because I do trust her and know that our relationship is strong.

What would I really do if something like pregnancy out of wedlock happened to one of my three daughters? It would be a shocker, but I pray that God would give me the grace to be the kind of accepting father He wants me to be. And I trust that He would give me the strength and the love to put my arms around my daughter and to see it through with her.

Acceptance Fosters a Secure Connection

It is so important for parents and youth leaders to learn and to practice acceptance of their young people. If we want our students to feel secure in our relationship, they need to feel that they are accepted for who they are. Insecure youth are seldom willing to be vulnerable. They will be much less apt to be transparent, meaning they will not share with you what is happening in their lives or what their friends have been doing and saying. When young people feel unaccepted and insecure, they live in fear—the fear that "I'll be rejected so I'd better keep my mouth shut."

That is why acceptance is indispensable in building a loving bond with the young people in your life, especially in the face of differences and conflicts. The more you communicate acceptance, the more likely they will be to remain open with you and to tell you what's happening in their lives. As you seek to nurture an intimate relationship with your young people based on acceptance, you will likely not face

> If we want our students to feel secure in our relationship, they need to feel that they are accepted for who they are.

the relational disconnection that characterizes this generation. Instead, you will get a positive response most of the time. It may not always be as obedient and sweet as you would like, but it will be a response made in trust, not fear, because your young people will know beyond all doubt that whatever happens and whatever they do, you love them for who they are—period!

CHAPTER 5

Connecting Point #3: Appreciation—Giving Youth a Sense of Significance

"Pixie Dust" by Dottie McDowell

As a little girl, my hero was Peter Pan. Just hearing the story took my breath away. I spent much of my playtime living and reliving each scene, and I couldn't get enough of it. Each time I dreamed about the boy who could fly, I felt inspired and energized.

I remember clearly the day I wandered down into our basement when I was about five years old. I spotted a box of Ivory Snow, a popular laundry detergent in those days, next to my mother's washing machine. In my well-developed imagination, each handful of soap flakes looked like the pixie dust that Tinkerbell sprinkled on Wendy, Michael, and John to enable them to fly. Thrilled at the prospect, I decided to relive the Tinkerbell scene. I'll never forget the exhilaration I felt as I took handfuls of "pixie dust" and sprinkled them generously throughout the entire basement. It was a magical moment in my young life.

When I was done, everything in the basement was covered with soap. Now let me ask you: If your child did this, what would your response be? When my mom discovered what I had done, she listened to my explanation, lovingly understood my childish fantasy, and recognized how much the experience meant to me. Instead of reacting in anger or frustration at the mess I had created, she laughed with me and encouraged me to repeat the whole story of Peter Pan to her. Later, still in a light-hearted mood, we cleaned up the enormous mess together.

What did this experience communicate to me? It assured me that my mom appreciated me and my wild imagination. What was important to me became important to her. She unselfishly chose to encourage my childish dreams while setting aside her own interests and convenience. I shall never forget it!

I was more than fortunate to have a mom who demonstrated appreciation for her children. She closely watched me, my brother, and my sister, and she studied our unique personalities. She knew what was important to each of us and embraced our individual dreams with enthusiasm and commitment. Each of us was a unique "favorite" to Mom and Dad. Since I was the eldest, I was their favorite big girl. My only brother was their favorite boy. And my younger sister was their favorite little girl. Josh and I have done the same thing with our own four kids. It changes often. This year, Kelly is our favorite medical student, Sean is our favorite son, Katie is our favorite blonde, and Heather is our favorite teenager.

Even as an adult, my mother would dream my dreams with me, wanting to know every detail and delighting in every interest that I pursued. Mom is with the Lord now. But did her interest in knowing the details of my pursuits communicate that she accepted me for who I am and appreciated what I did? You bet it did. Did her appreciation have a positive impact on my self-image—even as an adult? Absolutely!

THE BIBLICAL PRINCIPLE OF APPRECIATION

When we express appreciation to young people, we give them a sense of significance. While acceptance is the foundation for a secure relationship, appreciation can be considered a cornerstone. Our acceptance of young people tells them that their *being* matters. Expressing our appreciation to them says that their *doing* matters too. Appreciation gives people a sense of significance—feeling that they are valued and that their accomplishments do make a difference to some-

> Appreciation gives people a sense of significance.

one. It conveys the idea "Hey, I'm worth something to someone! These adults like having me around—and they're proud of me!"

Appreciation is a solidly biblical principle. When Jesus was baptized, His heavenly Father expressed appreciation by saying, "This is my Son, whom I love; with him I am well pleased" (Matt. 3:17). What was the heavenly Father doing? He was expressing appreciation to His Son. If the heavenly Father took time to express appreciation for His Son in front of the watching world, we should take time to appreciate our kids at home or in public.

The apostle Paul tells the Romans how much he appreciates them in Romans 1:8, and then he goes on to say specifically what he appreciated about them: "Your faith is being reported all over the world." Paul always expressed appreciation toward his "spiritual children" in the churches that he started. For example, Paul wrote to Timothy to say he constantly remembered him in his prayers and longed to see him because Timothy's sincere faith filled him with joy (see 2 Tim. 1:3–5). If Paul could take time to appreciate his protégés, we can take time to appreciate our protégés—the young people God has given us to train and nurture.

Unfortunately, a lot of people grow up without receiving appreciation and praise. They eventually learn to become suspicious of compliments, thinking that perhaps they are being set up. Consider trying this exercise with your young person. Stop one of them and say, "Hey, I need to talk to you."

> The more you praise your young people for what they are doing right, the less you have to criticize and discipline them for doing something wrong.

"Yeah, is there something wrong?" he or she may reply.

Then say, "No, I just want to tell you what a great job you did!" And then spell out what that great job was.

You will notice that the more you praise your young people for what they are doing right, the less you have to criticize and discipline them for doing something wrong. That's because praise becomes a motivator for proper behavior.

LEARNING TO BE A ONE-MINUTE FATHER

In my early parenting years, my approach tended toward catching my children doing something wrong and then disciplining them for their misbehavior. As a Christian father, I thought I had an absolute obligation, bordering on a grave responsibility, to correct practically everything they did. For example, if Dottie came into my office to report that Sean came home with straight As on his report card, I wouldn't interrupt my work to tell him, "Great job!" And by dinnertime I might have forgotten about it. But if Dottie interrupted me to say, "Sean is clobbering his sister," I would have said indignantly, "Send him in here right now. I want to talk to him."

I could give you countless examples of the same syndrome with my children in those early days. What I didn't realize was that I was teaching my kids something I didn't want to communicate at all: "The fastest way to get Dad's attention is to do something wrong." Today as I talk to young people across the country, I estimate that fifteen out of twenty kids tell me that is exactly how it is at their house. They can get the attention of parents and other adults much faster if they do something wrong.

Around 1984, when my kids were all under eleven years old, God spoke to me through—of all things—a book entitled *The One Minute Manager*.[1] In that book, authors Kenneth Blanchard and Spencer Johnson contend that managers can help their employees set and reach business goals if they apply a biblical principle of catching them doing something right and showing appreciation for their efforts. It was easy to apply the message to my parenting. Instead of seeing my job as a matter of catching my kids doing something wrong and correcting them, I learned how to relate to my children differently. My new motto was: Try to catch your kids doing something right and praise them for it. This didn't mean I wasn't going to deal with any misbehavior on my children's part; it simply meant I was going to outweigh any disciplining efforts toward my children many times over by catching them doing something right and praising them for it.

It's funny how a little phrase like that can bring a concept or principle to life. I was sold on giving my kids complete acceptance, but I had been struggling with learning how to appreciate them. One side of me had been trying to accept my children, and the other side had been trying to correct them for doing things wrong. It was no wonder that I often felt a little schizophrenic! But all that changed when I turned the emphasis upside down. Instead of concentrating on what they were doing *wrong*, I started making a conscious effort to look for what they were doing *right*. My new goal was to find at least two things about each child that I could appreciate every day and then to be sure to compliment each child on what I saw.

I'm not sure my kids noticed a change overnight, but I know I did. My whole perspective changed. When I saw Kelly studying, I would try to say, "Honey, I appreciate the way you study." When I saw Sean taking out the trash, I would try to stop him and say, "Sean, thanks for remembering to take out the trash." And when I caught little Katie picking up her toys, I would try to say, "Katie, sweetheart, Daddy really appreciates how you take care of your toys."

You might try this exercise. Gather your children or youth group in the same general area and stand in the middle of all of them for an "appreciation session." Think of at least one thing about each young person and share it out loud. This exercise will help remind you of just how much you have to be thankful for in your kids, and it will keep you primed for saying appreciative things at the proper time. You see, it isn't a matter of not being able to find things to appreciate about your kids; it's about disciplining yourself to *speak up and tell your kids what you see*—to give them honest praise for their effort.

I talk to parents who have the concept of parenting I used to have, and they say: "Well, kids are *supposed* to do certain things. Why should they be praised for something as ordinary as taking out the trash?" My response is, "Why not? How do you feel when you are praised for doing your jobs?" Anyone loves to hear the boss say, "I appreciate the way you handled that sale." Anyone who cooks loves to hear the family say, "That was great—you couldn't have fixed anything that would have tasted any better!" In the same way, your young people crave to be appreciated for even simple and expected chores or behaviors. For example, you can say things like:

- "Thank you for getting your homework done on time."

- "I appreciate it when you take your dirty dishes to the sink after we eat."

- "Thank you for putting the car in the garage for me without being asked."

- "I appreciate you for spending time with your little sister when you wanted to be out with your friends."

- "Thanks for always being on time for our youth group activities."

- "I appreciate your effort to make other students feel welcome in our group."

Recently a major national magazine reported on eight key things parents could do to keep their children excelling in school. One was "applaud the effort." Be specific and applaud your kids' efforts. Generic appreciation is good, but the more specific you are, especially applauding their quality of work and persistence, the greater the impact and the deeper it will connect you to your students.

HANDLE APPRECIATION WITH CARE

Having said all this about appreciation, here is a word of caution: Unless your young people are absolutely convinced that you accept them for who they are, your praise and appreciation can become manipulative. Appreciation without acceptance may prompt a student to relate to you on a performance basis, thinking, *If I do a good job . . . if I get As . . . if I score a goal . . . then my parents (or youth leader) will love me.* Living on a performance basis produces feelings of guilt.

> Unless your young people are absolutely convinced that you accept them for who they are, your praise and appreciation can become manipulative.

I often ask adults if they have ever felt guilty about failing at a task. Nearly every hand in the room goes up. "Why?" I ask. "What does failing at a task have to do with morality?" They get the point. When we fail at a task, we aren't really feeling guilt as much as we're feeling a sense of shame and self-condemnation. And that sense of self-condemnation drives us into being unwilling to accept ourselves because we are living on a performance basis.

That's why it doesn't hurt to bend over backward to make sure your kids feel first accepted *then* appreciated. For example, when your kids get their report cards, sit down with them and talk about what they achieved. Assure them that, while you appreciate their efforts to earn good grades, you always want them to know: "Even if you didn't get As, I would love you just as much and accept you just the same." Or when a core member of your youth group drops out of the leadership team, be sure to let him or her know, "Even if you can't be in leadership this semester, I still consider you a valuable part of our group."

Admittedly, there is a fine line to walk here. But the best way to walk that line is to keep acceptance of your young people as the foundation and build off that with appreciation. Make your students feel so secure and so accepted for who they are that they know you will love them whether they succeed or not. In other words: *Appreciate your students' efforts more than your students' accomplishments, and appreciate your students' worth as God's creation even more than your students' efforts.*

> Make your students feel so secure and so accepted for who they are that they know you will love them whether they succeed or not.

Could appreciating a young person's effort still be a "condition" that could push him or her toward living on a performance basis? That's certainly possible, but the best safeguard against that happening is constantly working to make your students feel accepted and then adding appreciation for their efforts.

OLD HABITS ARE HARD TO BREAK

If we let down our guard for even a moment, we can be right back to looking for what our kids are doing wrong and correcting them instead of first catching them doing things right and praising them. Trying to change is a lifetime job. There are usually two barriers to overcome. One is past habits. If we do not focus on taking the time to accept and appreciate our kids, we won't do it. If we don't keep the need to appreciate our kids in the forefront of our minds every day, we will let opportunities go by—and soon we won't be doing it much at all.

The second barrier is that Satan really does prowl about like a roaring lion (see 1 Pet. 5:8), and one of his most potent weapons is rationalization. We can easily tell ourselves, *My parents spent little time accepting and appreciating me, and I turned out okay.* But I would venture to say you really wish they had shown acceptance and appreciation to you. Besides, our kids are growing up in a different culture from the one we knew as kids. Our young people face pressures that didn't even exist when we were their age. They need all the help they can get.

But as long as we never stop focusing on accepting and appreciating them, our kids will know exactly what we mean when we urge them to do their best. And the continuously used channels of acceptance and appreciation will become like cords of love binding the hearts of our kids to ours in an intimate relational connection the culture cannot break.

CHAPTER 6

Connecting Point #4: Affection—Giving Youth a Sense of Lovability

It was an outdoor rally, so I stood on a boulder to be better seen and heard. There must have been about one thousand kids sitting on the grass at the Phoenix, Arizona, high school to hear my talk on love and sex.

Just as I got started, a group of punk rockers walked up and joined the crowd. The trend in those years was for punkers to dye their hair unusual colors and hang gold chains around their necks. And this particular group was in full regalia. Their arrival didn't cause much commotion, but because I had been warned that this group might try to cause problems, I kept my eyes on them as I talked. They just stood there, looking at me as if to say, "We dare you to say anything that we would want to listen to."

When my talk ended and I stepped down off the boulder, the leader of the punker group ran right up to me. This husky young guy came within inches of my nose, so most of the crowd neither saw nor heard what happened next. They didn't see the tears running down his cheeks or hear him politely ask me a poignant question: "Mr. McDowell, would you give me a hug?" Before I could even get my arms around him, the big punker grabbed me in a bear hug, put his head on my shoulder, and started crying like a baby. I hugged him back, and we stood there for almost a minute. I could tell he was sincere. He wasn't putting me or the crowd on. He really wanted a hug.

Finally, the punker stepped back and said something that I have heard from countless young people: "Mr. McDowell, my father has never once hugged me or told me he loved me." In his own dramatic style, this young man made a statement about the universal need for affection.

When we show affection to young people, we give them a sense of lovability. Expressing affection to our kids through loving words and appropriate touch communicates to them that they are worth loving. Every expression of care and closeness provides emotional reinforcement, helping kids realize that they are loved. As the apostle John says, "Let us love one another, for love is from God" (1 John 4:7 NASB).

THE UNIVERSAL NEED FOR AFFECTION

God created all human beings with a need for human affection, and this need is fully awake from birth. Medical research has established that an "infant's actual body temperature and growth hormones production are modified and regulated by the warm touch of a mother or caretaker."[1]

My friend David Ferguson, who is also a licensed marriage-and-family therapist, makes these comments:

During the nine months before birth, a child is enveloped by human touch in his mother's womb. From the moment of birth we reach out for the warm embrace of a mother's arms. From infancy through childhood and into adulthood the God-centered need for affection does not disappear. Touching somehow reconnects us with one another, makes us feel close, and removes our aloneness. No wonder Scripture instructs us to "greet one another with a holy kiss" (Romans 16:16), encouraging appropriate, physical affection among believers.[2]

Studies in state-run orphanages in Romania revealed that "persisting cognitive and emotional defects" occurred much more frequently in abandoned infants as compared to children raised in nurturing environments. Furthermore, a study of English and Romanian adoptees discovered:

Toddlers who were removed from Romanian orphanages before the age of six months and then adopted by dedicated families in the United Kingdom showed a remarkable degree of catch-up despite severe developmental deprivation on arrival.[3]

Family psychologist Kevin Leman teaches that we should never underestimate the power of a simple hug. In his book *Becoming the Parent God Wants You to Be,* he states:

One doctor studied 49 different cultures throughout the world to determine what effect physical affection and body touch have on children and adults. He learned that the more violent societies were the ones in which touching and caressing were rare in the family.[4]

> Affection communicates care and helps us feel close and connected to other people.

Affection communicates care and helps us feel close and connected to other people. This is as true for youth and adults as it is for infants and small children; we never outgrow the need for affection. If you desire to develop a deep and lasting emotional bond with your young people, you must show them appropriate affection.

Searching to Connect

The disconnected generation is not relationally disconnected by choice. Earlier, we documented the various ways kids today attempt to connect with others. Some gain a sense of connection with their peers through sports, clubs, gangs, or even schoolwork. The ways kids dress and decorate their bodies are often means to feeling connected to each other. But one of the most common ways young people reach out for an emotional attachment is through an affectionate relationship with a girlfriend or boyfriend.

In many respects, there is nothing wrong with seeking a measure of relational connection through peer activities or an appropriate romantic relationship. Forming connected relationships outside the home is part of God's design for His body, the church (see 1 Cor. 12). While this is not intended to replace the God-ordained parent/child relationship, children were meant to enjoy close relationships with others. For kids, relationships with others might include having fun with friends, participating in youth-group activities, playing team sports, or joining a club. Relational connections like these can be healthy and even reinforce the primary bond of affection between children and parents.

But when there is relational disconnection at home, young people may seek unhealthy means outside the family to fulfill their inborn but unmet need for affection. This heightened drive sometimes leads to an attempt to connect with the opposite sex, which can be a problem for three reasons. First, the changing hormones of puberty mean that kids' awareness of, and attraction to, the opposite sex is growing strong. Second, kids who are starved for affection at home may reach out to satisfy that need with peers to whom they are attracted.

> When there is relational disconnection at home, young people may seek unhealthy means outside the family to fulfill their inborn but unmet need for affection.

Third, a culture that glorifies sex and condones promiscuity can open the door for affection-seeking kids to become sexually involved. Ignoring a young person's need for affection can trigger an explosive and destructive chain reaction, leading to premarital sexual involvement and its frightening complications.

Numerous studies have documented the alarming rate of teenage sexual involvement and its devastating effects on the physical, spiritual, and emotional health of kids who are sexually active. I have personally invested more than twenty years in helping parents and churches equip their youth to say no to premarital sex and to develop the moral conviction to resist sexual pressure. This is why we launched the Why Wait? and Right from Wrong campaigns. I am fully in favor of teaching our youth to say no to premarital sexual involvement. Yet if I had to name one major reason that young people become sexually involved, I would say it is the lack of an emotional and relational connection between kids and their parents, especially their fathers. And a lack of affection almost always reveals a lack of connection.

Looking for Love in All the Wrong Places

Everywhere I travel and speak, I am confronted by young people who are starved for affection from their parents, especially their fathers. After a recent speaking engagement in New England, I received this note from a fifteen-year-old girl:

> Dear Josh,
>
> I watch your show every time I can. Thank you so much for just caring. The other night you said that most kids don't want to have sex, they just want someone to care. That is so true! I have almost fallen into the "sex trap" because I just wanted a man to love me.

Perhaps the most poignant letter I have ever received that represents this affection-starved generation is from a teenage girl. She sent me a letter along with a page out of her diary. As you read the following diary entry, imagine this young girl sprawled out on her bed. The door is closed and locked. A bed lamp dimly lights her page as she begins to write:

> August 11
> Dear Diary,
>
> I felt lonely tonight. And I thought about the many times in my life that I have felt lonely, intense loneliness, as though I

were here all alone. And I realized that what I was lonely for was a daddy—to be able to call him up when I hurt and hear him say he understands and know he listens to me. But I never had that with my dad. And so I am lonely without that link to my past. And then I thought about the young girl who this very night will lose her virginity because she is searching for love, her daddy's love. And I want to be able to stop her somehow and tell her that she'll never find it in another man. How my heart is wrenched when I think of this girl . . . when I think of myself. For my life has been one big search for my daddy's love.

Here's another letter:

Dear Josh,

My name is Frank, and I'm sixteen years old. I was touched by your talk today. I have a father, but my parents are divorced. Yes, I still see my dad. But he treats me more like an acquaintance rather than being a father to me.

I could fill the rest of this book with letters from young people who are crying out for love and sharing the tragedies they have suffered from their misplaced affections. Many of them have confused the intimacy of love with the intensity of sex. Longing to feel truly loved, they gave their bodies to someone and woke up with an empty heart the morning after. If you read the hundreds of letters I have received from young people, you would see a clear pattern. Kids are searching for the love and affection their parents have failed to provide, and their search often ends in sexual involvement and heartache.

When kids tell me about a lack of love at home, they most

often talk about their dads. I don't report this to condemn fathers. But the overwhelming evidence from sociological studies, plus my own research and experience with thousands of young people over the years, points to the indisputable conclusion: Today's young people miss a sense of love and affection from their fathers—and the consequences are tragic.

> Today's young people miss a sense of love and affection from their fathers—and the consequences are tragic.

Not long ago I wrote a book entitled *The Father Connection* to help dads connect with their kids. I want to share with you the following edited excerpt from that book, which documents the vital importance of two loving parents in the home and shows what happens when fathers are not there for their kids.[5]

THE FATHER CONNECTION

The role of the loving, involved father is critically important in the home, and it has never been more so than among today's disconnected generation. Study after study demonstrates that the father/child relationship is a decisive factor in a young person's emotional health, development, and contentment. Consider the following:

- Dr. Loren Moshen of the National Institute of Mental Health analyzed U.S. census figures and found the absence of a father to be a stronger factor than poverty in contributing to juvenile delinquency.

- A group of Yale behavioral scientists studied delinquency in forty-eight cultures around the world and found that crime rates were highest among adults who as children had been raised solely by women.

- Dr. Martin Deutsch found that the father's presence and conversation, especially at dinnertime, stimulate a child to perform better at school.[6]

- A study of 1,337 medical doctors who graduated from Johns Hopkins University between 1948 and 1964 found that lack of closeness with parents was the only single common factor to hypertension, coronary heart disease, malignant tumors, mental illness, and suicide.[7]

- A study of thirty-nine teenage girls suffering from anorexia nervosa showed that thirty-six of them shared a common trait: the lack of a close relationship with their fathers.

- Johns Hopkins University researchers found that "young, white teenage girls living in fatherless families . . . were 60 percent more likely to have premarital intercourse than those living in two-parent homes."[8]

- Dr. Armand Nicholi's research found that an emotionally or physically absent father contributes to a child's low motivation for achievement, inability to defer immediate gratification for later rewards, low self-esteem, and susceptibility to group influence and to juvenile delinquency.[9]

These findings correspond closely to recent research among youth in evangelical Christian churches. Our own survey of 3,795 churched youth showed that 54 percent of teens and preteens in evangelical church families say they seldom or never talk with their fathers about their personal concerns (compared to 26 percent who say they seldom or never talk with their mothers about such things). One in every four young people surveyed state that they have *never* had a meaningful conversation with their fathers. More than two in five (42 percent) say they seldom or never do something special with their fathers that involves just the two of them. And one in five say their fathers seldom or never show their love for them.[10]

At the same time, our study revealed that youth who are "very close" to their parents are:

- more likely to feel "very satisfied" with their life
- more likely to abstain from sexual intercourse
- more likely to espouse biblical standards of truth and morality
- more likely to attend church
- more likely to read their Bible consistently
- more likely to pray daily

These sobering statistics *do not* mean that mothers are unimportant. On the contrary, they underscore that, in most cases, Mom has been there all along, caring for, talking to, and spending time with the children. As a result, kids seem to *expect* Mom to be accessible, loving, communicative, and accepting.

With Dad, however, the law of supply and demand comes into play. In many homes, he is *less* accessible, *less* involved, or *less* communicative than Mom is. Since a father's time and attention are in short supply, children assign greater significance to their relationship with Dad. Kids crave what is withheld from them, and too often what is withheld is a close relationship with their fathers.

Dads, this is why the father connection is more critical than ever for your children. They are looking to you for a sense of authenticity, security, significance, and lovability in their lives. I hope that you will make every effort to nurture an emotional and relational connection with your kids, because they really do need you now.

When Affection Does Not Come Naturally

Many parents—especially dads—have told me how difficult it is for them to express affection to their kids. Some admit that they feel awkward showing any outward affection. Dads sometimes say, "My father never hugged me or told me he loved me, so I guess I turned out like him." If you find it difficult to show outward affection, I don't want to minimize your struggle. It may take time to work through some emotional baggage and get over the awkwardness of being affectionate, but it can be done. I know, because I also grew up without a father's affection.

As a child, I never knew a father's love or benefited from a father's example. I can't remember a single time when my father took me somewhere alone and spent time with me. Although I became a father after a less-than-perfect example in my own father, I have been blessed to know and learn from a series of models and mentors through the years. Chief among these has been my wife, Dottie, who was raised in a loving home. I have also learned much from Dick Day, who is (next to my son, Sean) the closest male friend I've ever had.

I met Dick when we were both attending seminary during the '60s. Dick is a few years older than I am, so at that time he was already married with four children. Like me, he was the son of an alcoholic father and the product of a dysfunctional home. He had come to Christ in his late twenties and entered seminary in response to God's call to the ministry.

We became close friends, and I was soon a virtual member of the Day family. Often I would show up at odd hours—like 6:30 A.M. or after 11:00 P.M.—eager to talk about something I thought just couldn't wait. Dick was always patient, kind, and loving— traits I knew little about while growing up.

I was impressed immediately by how Dick and Charlotte treated their children and each other. They had a rich and rewarding relationship with each of their four children. I was amazed at the fun they had—smiling, laughing, and hugging each other. (In fact, I really learned how to hug by hanging around with the Days!) I saw in Dick a clear, concrete model of the kind of father I wanted to be someday.

> The more you are in the company of affectionate people, the more comfortable you will feel about showing affection.

If you find it difficult to express affection and to connect emotionally with your kids because you lacked models in the past, I encourage you to find positive role models of affection who may be available now. Look for couples who are caring and affectionate to each other, to their children, and to people in general. Let their loving words and actions rub off on you. The more you are in the company of affectionate people, the more comfortable you will feel about showing affection.

How to Show Affection to Your Youth

There are three excellent ways you can show affection to your children. First and foremost, you can convey affection to your kids by being affectionate to one another as husband and wife. Second, you can express affection *verbally* to your kids. Third, you can demonstrate affection *physically* to your kids.

Be Affectionate in Your Marriage

I am convinced that children feel loved and cared for when their parents are openly but appropriately affectionate in the home. As Mom and Dad demonstrate a loving marriage relationship through hugs, handholding, kisses, kind words, and considerate care for one another, their children benefit from the emotional warmth.

When our daughter Kelly was younger, I used to ask her, "Kelly, do you know that I love your mother?" She would smile and reply, "Yeah, I know it."

"How do you know?"

"Because you always tell her."

"What if I lost my voice and couldn't tell her? How would you know then?"

"Because you always kiss her."

"What if I got chapped lips and couldn't kiss her? How would you know then?"

"Because you always hug her."

"What if I broke both arms and couldn't hug her? How would you know then?"

Then Kelly would give me the answer I was looking for: "Because of the way you treat her."

That's always the acid test. How do I treat my wife? I can be affectionate to her and give her a peck on the cheek as I rush out the door. But how I treat her as my children are watching every moment will tell the real story. If your physical expressions of affection as a couple are backed up by true love for each other, your kids will find emotional security in your marital relationship. The more your children see your love and devotion demonstrated, the more they will sense that you truly love each other. And the more secure your kids feel about your love for each other, the more likely they will be to connect with both of you.

> The more secure your kids feel about your love for each other, the more likely they will be to connect with both of you.

In Ephesians 6:1–4, we find a capsule description of how to have a connected family. Children are to obey their parents, and parents—fathers, especially—are to nurture their children wisely, lovingly, and fairly. But look back to Ephesians 5 for a moment. What is the context for this connected family? Husbands are to love their wives as Christ loved the church (see v. 25). They are to love their wives as they love their own bodies, for, Paul states, "he who loves his wife loves himself" (v. 28). Wives are to respect their husbands (see v. 33). The context of Paul's admonition that a child obey his parents is the supposition that the child lives in a home where his parents mutually love and respect each other.

Physical affection is part of that loving picture. Don't be shy about displaying physical affection around your kids. Dottie and I have always been openly affectionate to each other around our children. This may surprise you, but we have even communicated to them in appropriate ways that we are still on our honeymoon. And they know that we are committed to each other for life. After talking to thousands of kids across the country, I know that one of their greatest

> One of the most significant heritages you can leave your children is your love for their mother or father.

fears is that Dad is going to divorce Mom or vice versa. One of the most significant heritages you can leave your children is your love for their mother or father.

Let your affection for your spouse come through verbally as well as physically. Because I'm on the road a lot, I call home practically every night. Naturally, I want to talk to everyone. One of the kids usually answers, and after talking to Heather, for example, I will say, "Honey, it's good talking to you, but is that fantastic mother of yours at home? Is that good-looking woman I'm married to there? Would you let her know that her hubby is on the phone?" I may be in a hotel room in Russia or England or stuck in an airport in Boston or Los Angeles. But through the miracle of communications technology, I can convey to my children on a daily basis, "I'm committed to your mother." Every time I call home, I am reinforcing this vital principle: My children can feel connected and secure in the knowledge that I love their mother.

Small gifts to your spouse, sometimes given through your children, are another way for them to sense affection. Purchase a gift for your spouse, but deliver it in care of one of your children. Say something like, "Please give this to your mom. Slip it to her as a special gift from her husband" or "Surprise Dad with this gift from his lover."

Why go to such efforts? Because as you include your kids in your affectionate deeds, they become active participants in your love for your spouse. By including them in your expressions of love, they feel the love too.

Youth leaders, you also have an important role in demonstrating your love for your spouse in front of your students. Many of the young people in your Sunday-school class or youth group do not come from affectionate homes, and they are watching closely how you interact with your spouse. As you model kindness, gentleness, and genuine love for your mate, you will provide a positive role model for these students' future relationships.

Express Affection Verbally

Kids need to hear affectionate words from their parents, and they need to hear them often. They need to hear you say "I love you" with sincere devotion. Obviously, if you rattle off these three words like a commercial one hundred times a day, they will lose their impact. Affectionate words must come from the heart.

Be creative and look for ways to express affection beyond just saying "I love you." One variation is to catch your child's eye, wink at him or her, and mouth the words silently, "Hey, I love you." Use other affectionate expressions like: "You're really special"; "You're the best"; "You add so much joy to my life." And do not just *speak* your words of love. Use every means at your disposal: greeting cards, notes taped on a bedroom door, e-mail, voice-mail messages, a handwritten letter—even a small ad in the local newspaper. Be creative, but be sincere.

Some parents choose affectionate nicknames for their kids to affirm one of their unique qualities. Using an endearing nickname like Sweet Girl, Mr. Marvelous, Smiley, Bright Eyes, etc., at various times can serve to reinforce a kid's sense of lovability.

Youth workers, you can also verbally express your affection for the students in your youth group by sending them encouraging cards and e-mails, slipping notes in their Bibles or book bags, or telling them, "You are a really special kid, and I'm glad you're in our group."

Demonstrate Physical Affection

The physical connection of appropriate loving touch somehow strengthens the emotional connection between parent and child. Hugs and kisses, gentle pats, an arm around the shoulder, even playful tussling are common forms of physical affection. Physical touch alone will not supply the emotional connection, but it is difficult to maintain a loving emotional bond without the reinforcement of physical affection.

Older children and teenagers may act as if they don't need or want a lot of physical affection. Don't believe it. Your child's inborn need for a loving touch may change a little during adolescence, but it never goes away. However, you may need to discover more timely and acceptable ways to demonstrate your affection in order not to embarrass your child. You may want to be careful not to overdo your affection

> Your child's inborn need for a loving touch may change a little during adolescence, but it never goes away.

with your kids in front of others. But your private hugs and kisses can turn your child into a very affectionate young adult.

As our son, Sean, approached his teenage years, Dottie kindly warned me that he might not be as affectionate toward me as I would like him to be. After all, he was transforming from a little boy into a young man, and a lot of guys don't like to show affection. But it never happened. Sean has always been affectionate toward me. But if I hadn't been affectionate to him as a baby, it would be difficult for him to be affectionate as a teenager. Even in high school, when I came to see him on campus, Sean would run up to me, hug me, and kiss me on the cheek—whether his friends were around or not. Our close physical contact over the years has facilitated a warm and loving bond between us.

As youth workers, you can demonstrate appropriate physical affection for your students. Take every opportunity to express your care for them through a pat on the back or (for same-gender students) a friendly hug or arm around the shoulders. It is likely that a number of your young people are from broken homes or are emotionally neglected by their parents, and you can be an instrument of God's love by giving them the affection they need.

There is awesome power in simple but heartfelt expressions of verbal and physical affection. It is the power to strengthen the intimate relational connection between you and your young person as so many other forces in our culture try to tear you apart.

CHAPTER 7

Connecting Point #5: Availability—Giving Youth a Sense of Importance

The pressure was on. The book deadline was fast approaching, and I needed to focus on writing and editing. Although the memory of this experience takes me back some twenty years, I recall it vividly. I was right in the middle of editing a chapter when two-year-old Sean wandered in.

"Want to play, Daddy?" he chirped expectantly.

As an "experienced" parent (we had already been through the two-year-old stage with Kelly), I should have realized that Sean really only wanted a hug, a pat, and a minute or two to show me the new ball he was carrying. But I was working on an important chapter and felt that I just didn't have even two minutes to spare.

"Son, how about a little later?" I replied. "I'm right in the middle of a chapter."

Sean didn't know what a chapter was, but he got the message. Daddy was too busy, and he'd have to leave now. He trotted off without complaining, and I returned to my manuscript. But my relief was short-lived. Dottie soon came in and sat down for a "little chat." (My wife never tries to nail me; she has much gentler—and more effective—methods of correction.)

She began, "Honey, Sean just told me you were too busy to play with him. I know that this book is important, but I'd like to point something out."

"What is that?" I asked rather impatiently, because now my wife was keeping me from my all-important project.

"Honey, I think you have to realize that you are always going to have writing to do, and you are always going to have deadlines. Your whole life will be researching and doing other projects. But you're not always going to have a two-year-old son who wants to sit on your lap and ask you questions and show you his new ball."

"I think I hear what you're saying," I said, "and you make a lot of sense as usual. But right now I've got to finish this chapter."

"All right, Josh," she said. "But please think about it. You know, if we spend time with our kids now, they will spend time with us later."

I did think about it, and the more I thought, the more Dottie's gentle words were like a knife slicing me to the core. She was right. I would always have deadlines to meet, contracts to fulfill, phone calls to answer, people to see, and trips to take. But my children would only be children for a short time. Soon the years would sweep by. Would I have any more time for them next year than I did this year?

I knew what the answer would be if I didn't change my ways. Quietly, without any big speeches or fanfare, I made a decision. Ever since, I have tried to place my children ahead of my contracts, deadlines, and the clamor of a world that wants me to get back to them ASAP. For more than twenty years, I have done my best to make my family my number-one priority.

AVAILABILITY SAYS, "YOU ARE IMPORTANT"

I'm a goal-oriented person, so I'm not content unless I'm engaged in four or five major projects at once. But I always want my kids to know that I have time for them—that no person, activity, or thing is more important to me than my family. And they need to know that my first love, Jesus Christ, is the very foundation of my love for them and their high priority in my life. Jesus said, "Let the little children come to me, and do not hinder them" (Matt. 19:14). Christ as our example made time for young people, and we must as well.

When we make ourselves available to young people, we give them a sense of importance. And when we're not available, we are saying, in essence, "Oh yes, I love you, but other things still come ahead of you. You are not *really* that important." Expressing affirmation, acceptance, appreciation, and affection to our youth is critical, but we can only do that if we make ourselves available to them. Being there when your young people need you will not only tell them they are important to you; it will keep you relationally connected to them.

We all live busy lives. Even our own kids (53 percent) say their lives are too busy.[1] I realize that it is not easy to spend large quantities of time with our families. But it may shock you to find just how little time we do spend with our kids. Our study shows that 66 percent of our churched youth spend an average of less than four and one-half minutes a day with their fathers and 62 percent spend an average of a little more than eight and one-half minutes a day with their mothers.[2] That compares to a minimum of four hours per day teens spend with various forms of mass media.[3] It is difficult to convey just how important our kids are to us when the media take up twenty-six to forty-eight times more of our kids' lives than we do. If we want our kids to feel more important and connected to us, we simply must give them more of our time.

> If we want our kids to feel more important and connected to us, we simply must give them more of our time.

To better grasp the concept of a person's sense of importance related to another person's availability, imagine this scenario. You are a good friend of the boss at your company. One Friday, you need to see him on short notice. So you go to his office and ask his secretary if you could talk to him for just a few minutes. The secretary tells you, "I'm sorry, but he's totally booked up until next Tuesday. You'll have to come back."

Because you really need to see your boss now, you tell the secretary, "Look, I won't take much of his time. Please just tell him I need to see him. It will only take a minute." And then suppose the secretary calls your boss and tells him you're there. She mentions your name, but all she hears back is, "I'm sorry, I simply cannot see him now. He'll have to come back next Tuesday."

Now, how would you feel? You would likely feel less important or not important at all to your friend the boss. You might begin to think, *If only I were a vice president or regional manager or somebody who really mattered, he would see me.* The bottom line is that you would think, *I'm not important enough.*

That's exactly how our kids feel when we tell them the equivalent of, "Sorry, come back next Tuesday." It takes time and effort to make people feel important. As a youth worker, you may need to make yourself available to your students on your "off-duty" hours. If your young people sense that you are only available to them during church services or other youth-group activities, they may doubt that you sincerely want to have a relationship with them. Whenever possible, invite your students to your home or call them during the evenings to reinforce your desire to build a relationship with them.

It may be inconvenient to make yourself available when you are right in the middle of something. Granted, there are those times when you simply can't stop what you're doing. For instance, you can't drop everything to play video games or listen to music with your kids. But there are many times when you can interrupt your schedule if you want to and be available to your young people. Allowing such interruptions will help your kids realize that you think they are important. And when one of those uninterruptible times occurs, it won't have the same negative impact that it might if your young person consistently gets the message, "I'm too busy; come back another time."

Due to the nature of my worldwide ministry, I am on the road more than I am at home. Therefore, I have to really put in special effort to spend time with my wife and kids. I simply don't get to spend as much time with them as I would like. But I have learned a couple of things that have helped me emphasize my availability to my family.

The first one I learned was from Dottie. She said to me once, "Josh, I know you can't be with me every time I want you to be. But it helps me to know that you would be with me if you could." During those unavoidable times when my schedule takes me away from home, it is important that Dottie knows that I would rather be home with her. So now I share that with my family regularly. When I leave for a trip or call home while on the road, I say something like, "I'm sorry I can't be with you, and I really wish I could be. I want to be with you more than anything." It's not the same as being home, but it helps communicate my desire to be available even when I can't be.

Another thing I have learned to do is to have one of my kids meet me out on the road for a weekend when I am traveling. I recently had to apologize to Heather for overbooking myself and not leaving enough time for her. Then I arranged for her to fly out to meet me and spend a few days with me on tour. It's not the same as spending time with her in her world, but it does let her know that her dad wants to spend time with her.

KIDS SPELL LOVE T-I-M-E

If we say we accept our young people, show that we affirm them, say we appreciate them, and show them affection but spend little time with them, we might as well be like the noisy gong the apostle Paul talks about in 1 Corinthians 13:1. In other words, all our talk about how much we love our kids won't ring true unless we actually take the time to express our affirmation, acceptance, appreciation, and affection.

> Many adults are not available to the young people in their lives because they are just too busy with their own lives.

Unfortunately, many adults are not available to the young people in their lives because they are just too busy with their own lives. Everyone jokes about the hectic pace of life. But the jokes aren't funny when kids feel disconnected and alone because parents and other adults are overcommitted to other things. Adults often complain to me about having too much to do then tell me about their work schedules, church activities, and social lives.

These same adults try to tell me they spend "quality time" with their students. I'm convinced that one of the biggest myths going today is the myth of quality time. Of course we all want quality moments with our young people. But you don't get them by appointment or on some kind of tight schedule. You get quality moments by spending larger quantities of time with your kids. Out of the quantity comes the quality. We must have both!

One of the biggest advantages of quantity time spent with young people is that you are able to serve as a role model for them. Whenever you run an errand, try to take one of your students with you. Otherwise, you might miss an opportunity to model for them. It's when they are with us, their parents and youth leaders, that they can see how we respond to the world: how we act when another driver cuts us off or when somebody irritates us in some other way. Our kids will never know unless they are with us, watching us, experiencing these same frustrations with us.

Another myth we fall victim to is the one that says, "It's the big moments that count." You might call them the Disneyland experiences—those major excursions that take all day and usually cost a lot of money. For parents, these "big moments" include trips to an amusement park, movie theater, or zoo; for youth leaders, activities such as ski trips or youth camp. I used to believe that it was the big moments that counted with my kids, so I would haul them off to someplace to show them a good time. Finally, Dottie got through to me in her quiet but laser-accurate way: "Honey, it's not the big times they are going to remember. It's the consistent small moments that will mold them. That's what they are really going to remember."

She's right. Disneyland experiences are still on our schedule from time to time. But they are not as big as they used to be. Big moments are necessary, but they can never replace the consistent little moments of being with them. That's when your young people most feel loved—when you express your affirmation, acceptance, appreciation, and affection.

Here's another myth about relating to teenagers that must be dispelled: "The formative years are past." Many mistakenly believe that as children enter adolescence, they don't need their parents and other adult authority figures as much. They think the primary formative years are over as teens are branching out and becoming independent. There is some truth to this, but it's not the whole truth by any means, especially when you consider the continuing brain development at this age.

I can recall mentioning to Dr. James Dobson a few years ago that I had run across many parents who thought it was good to spend time with their kids when they were small, but once they got into adolescence, it wasn't as necessary. Dr. Dobson's reply was something like, "No, that's not right. According to my research, when children reach puberty, they need their parents—especially their fathers—just as much, if not more, than they ever did."

That brief conversation gave me new motivation to spend as much time as I could with my own teenagers and to keep encouraging other parents and adult authority figures to do the same. Yes, I realize it's not always easy. In fact, in many cases it can seem impossible. When I mention that young people need time with their parents and other caring adults, many moms, dads, and youth workers shrug their shoulders. "How can we spend time with our kids?" they want to know. "They have their own schedules, their own friends, and their own lives. They're almost too busy to talk to us."

I'm not talking about an approach to connecting to our kids that makes it seem like a life sentence—a daily duty that every adult must perform under duress. I'm talking about being someone who wants to nurture them at every opportunity, to strengthen those relational ties and help them feel connected to you. Spending time with your students is an absolute imperative if you

> Spending time with your students is an absolute imperative if you want to spare them from the pain and loneliness of the disconnected generation.

want to spare them from the pain and loneliness of the disconnected generation.

SEIZING EVERY MOMENT

Making ourselves available to young people does require time, obviously, but it also requires a relational mind-set. We can be around our kids and still not be available to them relationally. I've had many young people lament to me about their parents or youth leaders, "Even when I'm around them, it's like they're not there for me."

Seize the moments you have with your kids. Learn the art of asking questions. When you're riding in the car together or sitting at the table for lunch, ask questions. Go beyond, "How was your day?" or "Did you have any tests?" Go for some unique questions like:

- What have you always wanted to do that we've never done together as a family (or youth group)?

- If you could change our family (or youth group), how would you change it? (You might want to brace yourself for the answer.)

- If you were the father or mother (or youth leader), what would you do differently? (Again, you might want to brace yourself.)

- What makes you happy?

- What makes you sad?

- If you could ask God one question, what would it be?

- If you had a million dollars, what would you do?

- If you could visit any place in the world, where would you go?

Asking your youth questions not only tells them you're available to them, but it also gives you an insight into your students' world. The more they sense that you are interested in what they think and feel, the more important they will feel and the more connected they will be to you.

Now Is the Time

Some of the saddest words ever spoken are, "If only I had spent more time . . . if only I had listened to my kids more . . . if only . . ." Dottie and I have both heard these heartbreaking words many times.

When Heather was a baby, Dottie was on a trip with her alone. On the plane, they sat beside a kind lady in her sixties. She kept saying things to Dottie like, "Enjoy that baby!" and "Be sure you spend lots of time with her." Then she related a story that revealed to Dottie the reason for her words.

The lady explained that she had two sons, very close in age. She told of the mess her boys frequently made in her house and how it often drove her crazy. She confessed that she would sometimes dream about the day they would leave for college because the house would finally be clean.

With a painful look in her eyes, she described the day both of her sons left for college. She said that she went upstairs to their room after they had packed up and gone. The room was spotless—finally. Everything was in the right place. But it was too quiet. Her eyes filled with tears as she reminisced and said to Dottie, "I threw myself across one of their beds and sobbed." It didn't matter to her anymore that their room was clean. She shared that she just kept wishing she had more time with her sons. She urged Dottie again to fiercely guard any time with her children, warning her how quickly that time goes.

I had a similar experience. The wife of a senior vice president of a huge construction firm heard me speak at a local church about being available to your children. Later, I ran into this woman in a restaurant. She mentioned hearing my talk, then she started to cry.

"I have to share something with you," she said hesitantly. "My husband just died. He was a million-dollar-a-year man. He traveled all over the world building and constructing things, but he never took time for his children, even when he was home. All his children turned against him, and when they were grown, they would have nothing to do with him. On his deathbed, he confessed to me that he was dying as one of the saddest men in the world. He told me, 'I gained prestige, but I lost my family. If only I had spent more time with my children.'" The sad story emphasized to me the importance of Dottie's wise comment when Sean was only two: "If we spend time with our kids now, they will spend time with us later."

This widow's words remind me of what Jesus said: "What good will it be for a man if he gains the whole world, yet forfeits his soul? Or what can a man give in exchange for his soul?" (Matt. 16:26). Having more time for your kids will not gain your salvation, but it does indicate how seriously you take the clear advice from Scripture about being a faithful, loving, and nurturing parent or youth leader.

CHAPTER 8

Connecting Point #6: Accountability—Giving Youth a Sense of Responsibility

In chapter 2, we discovered the equation *Rules – Relationship = Rebellion*. In this chapter, we will consider the reverse: *Relationships – Rules = Irresponsibility*.

To connect relationally, we need to show our young people affirmation, acceptance, appreciation, affection, and availability. Yet, if we do not balance these relational connecting points with loving limits and boundaries, young people will not learn responsibility.

Scripture states that "each one of us shall give account of himself to God" (Rom. 14:12 NASB). **When we provide loving accountability to young people, we give them a sense of responsibility.** Accountability gives parameters in which a young person can operate safely and securely. Young people need the loving authority of parents and caring adults as a solid basis on which to make responsible, right choices. Without parameters, there are only confusion and chaos.

Dick Day has given me much wise counsel in this area, as well as to other families, over the years. In a chapter of *How to Be a*

Hero to Your Kids, which Dick coauthored with me, he gave great insight on how to provide loving accountability within the balance of love and limits. With permission of the publisher, I offer edited excerpts from that chapter by Dick Day.[1]

A Balance of Love and Limits

If love is to be genuine and nurturing, it must include limits. When we feel God's love in our lives, we also sense His control or limits. The same God who demonstrates a sacrificial love also gives us His law. Truth—God's truth—encircles us and our families. God's truth does not entrap us; instead, it sets us free.

By its very nature, truth does have limits. Truth includes boundaries—fences, if you please. Without these fences, the truth is distorted and we have a free-for-all where anything goes.

Fenced Pastures Are Good for Sheep—and Young People

One day I (Dick) was out for a walk on the mountainside and came across a man who was traveling the United States in a covered wagon. He had stopped to graze his mules on a nearby meadow, and I struck up a conversation with him. It turned out that he was very experienced in raising animals, and I happened to ask, "What's the best environment for raising livestock, like your mules: open grazing land, a large fenced pasture, or a corral?"

Without hesitation, he answered, "Oh, the fenced pasture, by far."

"Why?"

"Because when animals get into that open grazing land, they get lost. Often they may be attacked by predators. Open grazing land is just too unsafe. And, if you put them into a corral, they always have to be provided for. They can't roam around and provide for themselves. But when you put them into a good fenced pasture, all that they need is right there, and they can still operate on their own."

After the man hitched up his mules and his covered wagon creaked on down the highway, I thought about our conversation and the fantastic analogy it suggests from Scripture. God has given us all we need in green pastures and still waters (see Ps. 23). And yet He has also given us fences—His perfect law of liberty and the truth that makes us free in Christ (see James 1:25; John 8:32). Fenced pastures are not only good for livestock; they make sense for how we are to instruct our kids as well, particularly in a culture that emphasizes relative thinking and the "anything-goes" philosophy.

That's why there must be parameters—absolutes that give stability and authority—in a young person's life. At the same time, there must be balance. I call the balanced approach to providing accountability to our kids the relational, or authoritative approach.

- Relational (Authoritative)—Correct balance of control and support. The relational approach communicates: "I'm listening. . . . I care about you. . . . I want to understand. . . . This time we'll do it this way because . . ."

There are three other approaches that adults sometimes employ, but each of them is counterproductive. They are:

- Autocratic—Strong control but little support. The autocratic approach communicates, "You'll do it my way, or else!"

- Permissive—Strong support but little control. The permissive approach communicates, "You can do anything you want."

- Indifferent—Little or no control and little or no support. The indifferent approach communicates, "I really don't care what you do."

THE AUTOCRATIC APPROACH

The autocratic adult is an "absolute ruler." To be autocratic, you don't have to rule with an iron hand with beatings and abusive behavior toward your kids. In fact, many autocratic parents give children "good homes." They feed and clothe them well, let them play with other children, and in short, seem to provide everything needed for a "normal" life—everything but enough relational love. While they may never beat their children, autocratic parents still reign as absolute rulers of their families. They are very big on rules but low on relationships.

> Living in an autocracy causes young people to react in one of two ways: flight or fight.

Living in an autocracy causes young people to react in one of two ways: flight or fight. When children choose *flight*, they typically withdraw and learn to go along and be obedient—on the surface. Inside, however, they are seething. Dr. Howard Hendricks, professor at

Dallas Theological Seminary, often tells the story of the child whose father told him to sit down. The child refused to sit down, so the father thundered, "Sit down, or I'll make you sit down!" The child sat down, but under his breath he muttered, "I may be sitting down on the outside, but on the inside I'm standing up!"

In other variations of flight, young people can crumble and take desperate measures because they can't take it anymore. In these cases, kids may become runaways and, in the worst possible scenarios, suicides.

When a young person chooses to *fight*, his anger is out in the open. He complains, talks back, and lashes out verbally and physically. In short, this young person rebels because the rules he must live under are not cushioned or filtered by a loving relationship with his parents.

When I was involved in marriage-and-family counseling, I often had to deal with autocratic parents who would finally come to me in desperation and say, "I don't know what to do with my kid. He's all over the place—he won't obey, he won't do his schoolwork, and he won't come home on time. I'm at my wit's end."

"Well," I would ask, "what are you doing?"

"Why, I'm grounding him, of course. No television, no allowance, and no car keys. When I say grounded, I mean *grounded*!"

I generally made it a policy never to tell parents what to do with their children, but in cases like this, I always had the same suggestion: "Would you be willing to let up on your rules and punishments and try working on your relationship with your child?"

"Let up on the rules? You don't know my kid. He'll go berserk!"

The next question was always, "Well, is your plan working?"

Most parents got my point. Obviously, their plan wasn't working, or they wouldn't be in my office for advice. Some of them would even take my suggestions and occasionally be able to change their ways. Many, however, would not. It's hard for autocrats to change. Their "absolute power" is just too important, and many are too insecure to let go.

THE PERMISSIVE APPROACH

The other end of the spectrum is the permissive adult, who is strong on support but weak on control. In this case, *love* overpowers *limits* and, again, there is a serious imbalance. You have probably heard about or seen permissive parents in action. Actually, the child is the one in action, while the parents simply stand and watch their child destroy flowerbeds, furniture, and the peace of the household.

Permissively parented kids often hold their parents hostage. They may refuse to take naps, resorting to temper tantrums and screaming until their poor parents are willing to grant them any wish to keep them quiet. Perhaps the little tyrant wants a glass of water, so his mother runs frantically to get one. But when she brings it, he pushes it violently aside because she wasn't fast enough.

Mother stands there, offering the glass of water and warning her son, "If you don't drink it by the time I count to five, I'm taking it away."

Naturally, the count of five comes and goes, and the child still hasn't taken the water. But as his mother walks away, the child screams again for a drink. Around and around the parent and child go, with the child in charge because the parent will not set limits and the child knows it.

Permissively parented children get their way a lot, but they are no happier than the children in the autocratic homes because the balance of *love* and *limits* is not there. Frankly, with a lack of limits, children will grow up thinking, *If my parents really cared about me, they'd be more interested in what I do. . . . They would say no sometimes. . . . I guess they don't really love me.*

The Indifferent Approach

In 1970, a young, unknown psychologist rocked the parenting and publishing world with a book entitled *Dare to Discipline*. Dr. James Dobson's message was, "It's okay to discipline your kids within a framework of love and affection. Children need to be taught self-discipline and responsible behavior, and it's okay to set limits."[2]

Dare to Discipline was a direct response to the permissive approach to parenting that had swept much of the nation, beginning with publications such as Dr. Benjamin Spock's book *Baby and Child Care*. But permissive parenting didn't start because of the advice of a book. Many parents who were permissive in the '40s, '50s, and '60s came out of a Depression background.

When better times rolled in the '50s, many of these parents vowed that they'd give their children everything they didn't have. In fact, they proceeded to have an extraordinary number of children, creating what is now called the "baby boom," which occurred between 1946 and 1964. These parents of baby boomers became, in many respects, indulgent.

It is no surprise that an indulged child is likely to become a self-indulgent adult. Children of the baby boomers, the so-called "me generation," became parents themselves—and, in many cases, they slipped into certain modes of indifferent parenting. In some homes, this indifference is glaringly evident, but in other families it's hard to spot.

I do not wish to make a wholesale indictment of the entire baby-boomer generation of parents. Many baby-boomer parents are involved with their children and are doing a good job. Nonetheless, the pattern is there. If you are a baby-boomer parent who was raised somewhat indulgently, you will no doubt need to focus on the issue of availability and come to grips with just how much time you have for your children and your spouse.

Be aware that it is entirely possible to provide a nice home, to buy the kids all the nice things of life, and still be unavailable to them physically and/or emotionally. Indifference can be communicated in very subtle ways. And when young people sense they are being parented indifferently, they become hurt and angry. Indeed, this generation has become the "hurt and angry generation," who will undoubtedly continue a pattern of dysfunction when they grow up, marry, and have children of their own.

I know from personal experience how the pattern of dysfunction can occur. I grew up in a home in which my parents had divorced but later remarried. Due to the pressures of my dad's job as an executive vice president, he and my mother moved in fast circles where drinking was common. Eventually, they became "functioning alcoholics."

I knew intellectually my parents loved me, but they were so wrapped up in their own lives that they paid me little attention. To cope with my life at home, I withdrew—spending most of my time in my room listening to my radio and tuning out everything and everyone else, particularly studying. My family was so dysfunctional, I went through two semesters of my freshman year in high school with straight Fs. Yet no one—teachers or parents—seemed interested.

Finally, toward the end of my second term, my parents stopped long enough between cocktail parties to realize that they hadn't seen my report card all year long. When they did see it, they tried to take what they thought was "loving action"; the next year I was shipped off to a prep school to repeat my freshman grade.

I was well into my twenties, married, and with four small children when God intervened to save me and my family from what undoubtedly would have been a continuance of the cycle of dysfunction. When my wife and I became Christians, we vowed that the patterns of neglect that I'd known as a child would never be repeated—and they haven't.

THE RELATIONAL (AUTHORITATIVE) APPROACH

We have looked at three different approaches to young people that we want to avoid: autocratic, permissive, and indifferent. But what about the relational, authoritative approach—the ideal that we hope to reach? What does a relational parent look like? More important, what does the relational parent do while providing loving authority?

Volumes have been written on how to be an effective authoritative parent. But I have found no better description of the relational parent than a verse from one of Paul's letters: "And, fathers, do not provoke your children to anger; but bring them up in the discipline and instruction of the Lord" (Eph. 6:4 NASB).

What did Paul mean by "provoke your children to anger"? The New International Version says, "Fathers, do not *exasperate* your children" (emphasis added). J. B. Phillips translates this verse, "Fathers, don't *over-correct* your children or make it difficult for them to obey the commandment" (emphasis added). And The Living Bible says: "Don't keep on *scolding and nagging* your children, making them angry and resentful" (emphasis added).

With the different negative parenting styles in mind, one way to paraphrase Ephesians 6:4 could be, "Do not drive your children crazy with autocratic, permissive, or indifferent parenting. But, instead, build a loving, authoritative relationship, based on the parameters of God's Word."

So far so good, but how are we to do what Paul suggests in the second part of Ephesians 6:4, "bring them up in the training and instruction of the Lord"? Here are some basic principles for providing loving accountability to your children.

Make the Payoff for Misbehavior Small

It helps to remember that when young people do something wrong, they are usually seeking attention. Obviously, you cannot ignore your child when he or she misbehaves. You have to deal with the misbehavior, but the question is, *How* do you deal with it? What does the child see and hear as you respond to his or her misbehavior?

If the child can get the volume of your voice to go up, if he can get you red in the face, if he can provoke you in any number of ways, he will conclude that his misbehavior is the best way to get your attention.

On the other hand, if you can deal with his misbehavior quietly, without long, loud lectures or other angry outbursts, the payoff will not be nearly as big. One simple approach is to tell the child quietly that this kind of thing won't be tolerated and, if necessary, to separate him from the rest of the family for a while. Remember, it's harder to get attention when you're all alone. The "chair in the corner" method of correction may seem old-fashioned, but with many children it is extremely effective.

I realize that with some children it isn't that simple, but however you deal with your child's misbehavior, keep in mind that children are bound to do some things wrong. They are bound to misbehave on occasion simply because they are children. Make it your goal not to make such a big issue out of their negative behavior; instead, try to catch them doing something right instead of always looking for what they are doing wrong.

> You need a system of discipline that gives the child every chance to learn and to mature.

To do this effectively, you need a system of discipline that gives the child every chance to learn and to mature. I believe that Scripture teaches two modes of positive discipline that psychologists have "discovered" only in recent times. One is called "natural consequences," and the other, "logical consequences." Both are based on simple cause-and-effect principles.

Use Natural Consequences as Accountability

The parable of the prodigal son is an excellent illustration of natural consequences. The young man decided to leave home and live it up, and he demanded that his father give him his share of the inheritance. The father knew what would happen, but he handed the money over anyway to let natural consequences bring his son into account.

Natural consequences took their toll, and eventually the young prodigal wound up eating with the pigs because that was all he had. The key line in the entire parable is, "When he came to his senses . . ." (Luke 15:17). It took natural consequences to bring the boy to his senses. He decided to return to his father's house, where he was accepted and loved more than ever (see vv. 11–32).

I recall using natural consequences to teach my youngest son, Jonathan, an important lesson when he was very small. We had an open fireplace in our home that was at floor level, and I often worried about Jonathan. Not realizing what fire could do, he could reach into the fireplace and get terribly burned while my wife, Charlotte, and I weren't looking.

One evening we were sitting at dinner eating by candlelight, when Jonathan started to reach up to touch the candle flame. Charlotte started to stop him, but I said, "No, let him do it."

Jonathan moved his finger toward the flame then withdrew it immediately. He really didn't get burned, but he felt the flame just enough to learn the power of fire and to respect it. From then on, little Jonathan understood something about fire, and my fears of his getting near the fireplace were greatly diminished.

Use Logical Consequences as Accountability

The other mode of accountability described in Scripture is logical consequences. This simply means that the parent determines with the child that certain consequences will happen if the child does not fulfill his responsibilities in some way. For example, "If you don't eat all your dinner, you get no dessert" or "If you don't feed your puppy, you don't eat either."

We see the precedent for logical consequences taking place in the Garden of Eden with Adam and Eve. God laid everything out for them and then made it clear that the one tree they could not eat from was the tree of knowledge of good and evil. If they did eat from that tree, the logical consequence would be that they would "surely die" (Gen. 2:17).

Tempted by the serpent, Eve ate from the tree, and then Adam followed suit. When God discovered what had happened, the consequences came swiftly. Adam and Eve became susceptible to physical death and all its related penalties, such as pain in child-birth, living by the sweat of one's brow, and banishment from the Garden of Eden (see Gen. 3:1–19).

God had spelled out the boundaries in which Adam and Eve could operate, and when they chose to violate or to cross those boundaries, they had to face the consequences. Yet God did not set these limits until He had first demonstrated His love by pro-viding for their every need—physically, emotionally, relationally, socially, sexually, and spiritually. When He set limits, God was giving Adam and Eve an opportunity to respond to His love by trusting and obeying.

Parenting children works much the same way. Parents are responsible to spell out the boundaries for their children. By lay-ing down limits, you make the child accountable for his or her actions and behavior.

Parents and Christian Leaders Who Have Ears, Please Hear

When I was doing family counseling, a thirteen-year-old girl and her parents came to see me. The father was in a high-profile

Christian music ministry and traveled the country singing and giving his testimony.

As we talked, I made some observations that caused the father to proceed to give a beautiful theological dissertation—something very doctrinally sound about what the Bible says concerning the family. It was a beautiful speech, well calculated to impress me and to intimidate his wife and daughter.

When the father finished, the daughter turned to her dad, and, in a quiet, almost wistful voice, she said: "Dad, I wish you could have heard what you just said and do it."

This girl was not rebellious or disrespectful. She desperately wanted her family to be connected relationally, but her dad could not hear her. He was too intent on keeping his power and what he believed was "authority." His daughter was telling him that the real secret to authority is a servant's heart. The servant leader listens to his family and is always more concerned about relationships than rules. To be a servant leader, however, the one in authority must know more than how to bring someone into account. He must also know how to be affirming, accepting, appreciative, affectionate, and available.

> Relational parents hear the disconnected cries of their children and move toward them with a balance of love and limits to connect with them.

Jesus, the greatest servant leader of them all, said on several occasions: "He who has ears to hear, let him hear." Relational parents hear the disconnected cries of their children and move toward them with a balance of love and limits to connect with them.

A Note to Youth Leaders

Although the message of this chapter, adapted from *How to Be a Hero to Your Kids*, was originally written to parents, these leadership principles also apply to youth leaders and other adults who minister to young people. If you are someone who has a leadership role with youth, think of ways to balance love and limits in your attempt to connect relationally with them. Instead of being autocratic, permissive, or indifferent to your students, take a relational, authoritative approach to leading your youth group or Sunday-school class.

In Part Two, we have covered six relational connecting points: affirmation, acceptance, appreciation, affection, availability, and accountability. When applied, these connecting points will deepen our relationships with our kids. In Part Three, we want to discover more about our kids' world and how we can enter that world to make these relational connections.

PART 3

Connecting in Their World

CHAPTER 9

Connecting in Their World of Disappointments

Fifteen-year-old Tim is a whiz at tinkering with computers. He spent several weeks building an innovative processor for the high-school science fair. If his project had won the computer division, Tim would have been invited to the district science fair, where cash prizes were awarded to the winners. He really needed the money to replace his savings, which he had spent on parts for his project.

But Tim's project didn't win. After all the hours he had put in, Tim didn't even get an honorable mention in his division. Naturally, Tim was disappointed.

When he told his parents about the results of the science fair, Tim got little sympathy. "Well, I questioned whether what you were doing would really pay off, but I didn't say anything," his father muttered.

"It's not good for you to be locked up in your room with computers all afternoon anyway, Tim," his mother added. "You need to get outside and be with people more."

His father put in quickly, "And besides, I've heard there are a lot of temptations on the computer. What about those bad

Internet Web sites? I think we better cut back your computer time until you get caught up on your chores and other homework."

Tim's disappointment quickly sank to discouragement.

It took a couple of weeks of hard work after school for Tim to catch up on the work he had neglected while preparing his science-fair project. It felt good just to have an evening to sit down and play computer games.

When his dad came into his room, Tim hoped for a few words of appreciation for all he had accomplished. Instead, his dad gave him another chore to complete and an errand to run. When he got back to his computer an hour later, he discovered that his little sister had been playing with it and inadvertently crashed his hard drive. He complained heatedly to his parents, but they said it was no big deal, explaining that Carrie didn't mean to do it. Tim sat in his room alone. He had no computer, no money to fix the computer, and no job to earn the money he needed—and his parents said it was "no big deal." It *was* a big deal to Tim, but nobody seemed to notice—or care.

Things didn't get much better during the next few months. Tim did enough of his chores and schoolwork to keep the peace at home, hoping his parents would cave in and help him fix his computer. But every time he brought up the subject, they said something like, "You don't need your computer, Tim. See how much better you're doing without it?" Tim silently agonized that he was stuck in a hopeless Catch-22. He didn't see any way to convince his parents how much he wanted and needed to be working on computers. He felt alone, trapped, and hopeless.

During the next several weeks, Tim began to experience longer periods of feeling sullen and lethargic. He spent all his spare time in his room doing nothing. His grades began to plummet, and his parents leaned on him to work harder. They grounded him week after week, which suited Tim fine. He didn't want to go anywhere or do anything. He just didn't care anymore. He was experiencing real depression.

Meanwhile, Tim's computer buddies at school drifted away from him. Since Tim could no longer chat and play games with them on-line, they had nothing in common with him. Regarded as a computer geek by other students, Tim had no friends. Failing in his classes and ignored by his peers, he began cutting school to hang out at the video arcade. He swiped candy bars from a local gas station and sold them to kids so he could play video games. One day he got caught, and his parents went ballistic. They threatened to take him to their minister for counseling. If that didn't work, they would look for a child psychologist.

Tim wanted to run away, but he didn't know where to go. He had reached a point of despair.

His parents shuttled him to a series of counseling sessions, but Tim just shut down every time. He wouldn't answer the counselor's questions or listen to her advice. At home he felt like a prisoner. Every movement was observed or questioned. Every wish for privileges or favors was denied. It was not just a prison; it was death row, he thought. But what was there to live for anyway?

Tragically, the seed thoughts of self-destruction were falling onto fertile ground.

THE DOWNWARD SPIRAL OF DISAPPOINTMENT

The problem is that we often find out about many kids like Tim too late. They show up in hospital emergency rooms as suicides or attempted suicides. The agonizing question that burdens the parents, youth leaders, and friends of students who attempt suicide is, Why? Tim had a good home. His parents may have been a little overprotective and domineering at times, but their motives were good. They only wanted the best for their son. And Tim didn't grow up with a twisted sense of self-worth that predisposed him to suicide. How does a reasonably well-adjusted kid like Tim become so disconnected as to consider that life is not worth living?

It doesn't happen overnight, and I'm not suggesting that many—if any—of the young people in your life are seriously harboring thoughts of self-destruction. But it is important to understand how students arrive at this point, the bottom of a dangerous downward spiral, so the appropriate preventive steps may be taken long before they reach the bottom rungs. Let's look at the five steps in the downward spiral of a young person's world of disappointments.

Disappointment

As Tim's story illustrates, young people may be nudged into an emotional downward spiral when their disappointments are not acknowledged or addressed by the significant adults in their lives. Kids become disappointed whenever their hopes or expectations are not met. Most of the disappointments they experience are relatively minor, but each is an emotional downer that must be addressed.

"But Josh," you may argue, "every kid experiences disappointments—sometimes several each day. How can they avoid disappointments?"

I'm not saying that our duty is to *prevent* kids from experiencing disappointment. That would be an impossible task. I'm saying that we must be prepared to *deal with* the disappointments they experience in their day-to-day lives.

Tim was disappointed that his project did not win anything in the school science fair. In reality, there were scores of kids who were disappointed—perhaps the winners were the *only* kids not disappointed that day. But Tim's disappointment went unresolved when his parents failed to affirm his feelings and make a loving connection with him at

> If we fail to recognize their many disappointments, our kids may be drawn downward in the dangerous spiral.

that point. If we fail to recognize their many disappointments, our kids may be drawn downward in the dangerous spiral. The further down the spiral they tumble, the greater the disconnection and loneliness they sense.

Discouragement

Unresolved disappointments can lead to discouragement, which means deprivation of courage, hope, and confidence. When his expectations are repeatedly unmet over time and his pain is not healed, a student begins to lose heart. He fears that what he has been hoping for will never be attained. Tim grew discouraged when his parents restricted his access to the computer, which was his main source of fulfillment. Along with the discouragement came a greater sense of disconnection from his parents.

Depression

Extended or repeated discouragement may lead to depression in the form of sustained periods of gloominess, dejection, sadness, and withdrawal from others. The student's discouragement broadens and generalizes to other areas of his life. He begins to think that more of his hopes and expectations will not be fulfilled. Tim became depressed when it appeared that he might never get his computer back. It was as if his main interest and excitement in life were being taken away.

Despair

When problems block out all their hope, kids experience despair, the sense that life is totally hopeless. Proverbs 13:12 describes it this way: "Hope deferred makes the heart sick." Everything in Tim's life seemed to be a gigantic failure: his interests, his friendships, and his home life. Everywhere he turned, he saw opposition and futility. Tim may not have had a true picture of his situation, but the despair was real to him.

Destruction

As with Tim, for some students, it's a small step from utter despair to thoughts of self-destruction. If life is hopeless, why go on?

I'm really not an alarmist. I don't want you to think that your students are only steps away from the slippery slope that could result in a suicide attempt. They probably are not. Yet the depression and despair that characterize so many in the disconnected generation beg us to examine how we respond to the disappointment and discouragement kids experience. Then we need to enter their world and take appropriate steps to help hurting kids get reconnected so they are not sucked into the vortex of self-destruction.

WHAT DOES DISAPPOINTMENT LOOK LIKE?

A primary way to keep our kids connected with us is not to let them deal with their disappointments alone. When you notice that your student is feeling down, waste no time moving into his or her world with appropriate responses that convey your loving care.

> A primary way to keep our kids connected with us is not to let them deal with their disappointments alone.

How can you know when a student has been disappointed? What does disappointment look like in a student's life? I would like to sort student disappointments into two general and somewhat overlapping categories. First, there are disappointments that center on *things* or *experiences*. We will discuss this category in this chapter. Second, there are disappointments that center on *people* or *relationships*. We will discuss relational disappointments in the next chapter.

In order to determine in which area your kids are encountering disappointment, just take a close look at the activities they are involved in. The more involved they are, the more possibilities for disappointment they face. Let's consider several common arenas of adolescent activity and disappointment.

School

Kids today spend a significant number of hours each week in school and school-related activities. In addition to daily classes, they may be involved in clubs, student politics, intramural or interscholastic sports, debate team, dance, band, etc.

On any given day at school, a student may suffer several of the following disappointments:

- failing a test
- arriving at school or class late
- misplacing a homework assignment or textbook
- losing an election for a student body, class, or club office
- being demoted or cut from a team
- losing a game or competition or making a critical error
- failing to qualify for a desired position, team, or honor
- forgetting an important meeting or activity
- getting ripped off—book bag, calculator, Walkman, food money, etc.

Work and Money

Many students seek part-time jobs so they can have spending money to buy the things they want. Jobs, finances, and possessions supply the following common disappointments:

- losing a job or being unable to find a job
- realizing that a work schedule conflicts with social life
- failing to get a promotion, raise, or better working conditions
- having a bad day at work
- not being able to afford desired things—car, clothes, ski equipment, etc.
- receiving an unexpected bill or expense

Physical Appearance and Health

A student's self-image is dramatically affected by his or her appearance, so this arena can be riddled with any of the following daily disappointments:

- having a bad hair day

- suffering an illness or injury that limits activity

- being embarrassed by lack of coordination, skill, or attractive appearance

- being dissatisfied with physical attributes: body type, foot size, skin tone, etc.

- not having "cool" clothes, jewelry, or accessories

- being humiliated by comments about weight, dress, or general appearance

General Expectations

Any of the following disappointments fall into the category of general expectations that are not met:

- learning that a long-awaited trip or event is canceled

- receiving bad news of some kind

- breaking or losing something of value

- realizing that life "isn't fair"

These lists are just a few examples of the disappointments our kids encounter as they work through daily life. And each disappointment, if not noticed and addressed by those who care about the students, has the potential of causing even deeper pain. So it is important that you enter their world by watching carefully for the disappointing experiences in your kids' daily lives. It is equally important that you enter their world regularly to ask them about their day—without prying—to find out how they might have been disappointed when you were not with them. Don't just ask them about their activities; ask them how they *felt* about the activities they were involved in. As soon as you discover an area of possible disappointment and hurt, make a loving connection.

> As soon as you discover an area of possible disappointment and hurt, make a loving connection.

CONNECTING THROUGH AFFIRMATION

The most important initial response when young people struggle with disappointment is to affirm their feelings. It doesn't matter if the cause of the disappointment is the student's fault or not. In reality, the pain may be even deeper when the cause *is* his or her fault. For example, sixteen-year-old Rob may feel badly because another car crunched his car in a minor traffic accident. But the pain may be even greater if Rob's driving error was the cause of the accident. Resist the temptation to confront the youth immediately about any blame that may be his. Deal with the pain of the disappointment first, then deal with the cause of the disappointment as necessary.

As we have covered in an earlier chapter, affirming your young person's feelings often comes through comfort. Comfort is best expressed through loving words and touch. Verbalize your comfort in terms that convey your sadness and hurt for the student. Think about Tim again, the fifteen-year-old computer whiz. Upon learning about his disappointment over losing at the science fair, a comforting adult may have said something like, "I'm so sorry that your project didn't win, Tim. It's a painful disappointment, and it hurts, doesn't it? I hurt for you."

No matter what the disappointment may be, words of comfort should center on the fact that you recognize that the student is feeling hurt, that you are sad for him or her, and that you hurt because he or she hurts. If the student is hurt to the point of tears, it's okay to cry with him or her. As we have said before, mourning and weeping with someone is one of God's ways of helping to heal the hurt.

Comforting words can be underscored by appropriate comforting touch: a gentle pat on the shoulder, a hug, or holding a hand. Loving words and touch convey that you are with the young person in his or her disappointment. And when he or she senses that you have joined him or her in a world of disappointment, the sense of loving bond and emotional connection is made.

OTHER CONNECTING POINTS DURING DISAPPOINTMENTS

Comfort is our vital first response to young people who have experienced minor and major disappointments. Once you connect with them by sharing in their hurt or sadness, it is important to further strengthen the connection. Supplement your comfort with other connecting points of your love.

Acceptance

You communicate acceptance by delineating between the youth—whom you love without conditions—and the circumstance that caused his or her disappointment. Often the hurt can be traced to a failure or oversight on the youth's part. But it is critical that you treat the person and the cause separately. He is not a "dummy" for losing his math textbook; he is a great kid who did a dumb thing. No matter what young people do to cause a problem, you will strengthen your connection with them when you accept them as fully as if they were not at fault.

Instead of communicating acceptance to their disappointed son, Tim's parents criticized him for spending too much time and money on his computer project. True, some of Tim's priorities may have been out of balance. But at his low moment, he needed to be reminded that his parents loved him unconditionally more than he needed to be reprimanded for not staying up with his chores. They could have reaffirmed their acceptance by saying something like, "We're proud of you for entering the science fair. You did a fine job on your project. You are always in first place with us." The issue of Tim's time priorities and attention to his chores should be dealt with separately.

Appreciation

Young people sense our love when they know they are appreciated in the face of their feelings of disappointment and failure. What can you appreciate about something that caused your student disappointment? Compliment his effort, his hard work, his positive attitude, his noble attempt—any positive elements you can think of.

Another thing you can do in a young person's time of disappointment is to be supportive by lending a shoulder to help lift the burden of the moment in practical ways. If the student has lost something, you may want to help him look for it. If something is damaged or destroyed, offer to discuss with the youth how to repair it or to replace it. You may also provide loving advice or instruction aimed at helping the youth avoid this disappointment in the future. Such words, when offered in the context of your comfort and acceptance, will be more readily welcomed and heeded.

You can also help prevent disappointment from spiraling down into discouragement by helping your youth refocus on his goals. The shortstop who committed an error that caused his team to lose an important game may be so disappointed that he wants to quit baseball. Someone needs to be there with the encouraging words, "I enjoy watching you play ball. Just keep trying your best." The candidate who lost the election for student-body treasurer is waiting to hear, "You have a lot to offer in student government. What other opportunities are available this year?" Your encouraging words can communicate, "Don't give up. Keep trying. I'm thinking about you and praying for you. I'm your greatest fan."

Everyone deals with disappointments every day, including the students you love and interact with. They can't go through life without suffering disappointments of their own making or disappointments at the hands of others. But disappointments are not likely to degenerate into discouragement, depression, despair, or destruction if you make sure your kids don't go through their disappointments alone. Entering their world at connecting points such as comfort, acceptance, and appreciation will short-circuit the destructive downward spiral and strengthen a loving connection with you.

CHAPTER 10

Connecting in Their World of Relational Losses

Cathy was a Christian girl who had lived in the same foster home for several years. She loved her foster parents as if they were her birth parents. Cathy was actively involved in a church youth group in which she had lots of friends.

One summer, Cathy and her friends went away for a week at the church's youth camp. It had been a great week, and she couldn't wait to get home and tell her family all about it. But she was in for a big shock. When she got home, her foster parents tearfully announced that Cathy was being immediately transferred to a group foster home in another state. The authorities had made the decision independent of Cathy and her foster parents. The distraught family was powerless to do anything about it. Cathy left the next day.

When I heard about this incident, I cringed inside. In less than twenty-four hours, a sweet Christian girl lost her parents, home, church, and friends. How could anyone be so insensitive to this girl and her foster family? It must have hurt her deeply to be torn from her family and friends and taken to a strange environment.

In the weeks that followed, Cathy probably suffered the horrible pain of being disconnected from loved ones against her will.

The young people you know and care about may never experience a devastating separation like Cathy's. But every student faces relational loss or separation that brings inner pain. Kids form strong bonds with family members and close friends over the years. When these bonds are broken for some reason, young people are left with deep hurt that does not quickly heal. They need a caring adult to enter their world to connect with them at this point to help heal the inner wounds of relational separation.

> Every student faces relational loss or separation that brings inner pain.

THE PAIN OF RELATIONAL SEPARATION

In the previous chapter, we discussed disappointments as they relate to a student's expectations regarding *things* and *events*. In this chapter, I want to talk about disappointments as they relate to the *people* and *relationships* in a student's life. Even though the characteristics overlap in these two categories, disappointments resulting from relational separation seem to inflict the greater pain of a deep loss. For example, the pain and sense of disconnection and aloneness Cathy must have felt at being moved away from her family and friends were likely much greater than the pain of losing a favorite necklace or being cut from the volleyball team. So in this chapter, we will talk about helping kids deal with the loss of loved ones, a loss that may prompt a sense of disconnection.

Here are five settings in which young people may experience the disconnection and loss of separation from family members or friends: when they move or their friends move away, when friends reject them, when families split up, when a romance ends, or when friends or family members die. Let's look at each one closely to see how to best keep our kids from suffering the painful disappointment of separation and loss alone.

When They Move or Their Friends Move Away

As Cathy's story illustrates, a great sense of aloneness results when a student is separated from friends or family through a move. We don't know how successful Cathy was at coping with her loneliness and establishing new friendships after her sudden move. Even if everything worked out well for her in the new location, the move likely was a traumatic event, leaving her feeling insecure and uncertain about her relationships.

Darryl is an adult who told me of a very close friendship he had during the first two years of high school. Then Darryl's family moved, and he had to transfer to another high school. He never was able to establish the kind of intimate friendship he enjoyed before the move, and he still finds the lack of close friends a source of discouragement.

The separation of distance brings aloneness, and aloneness can prompt disconnection. It is another important time for loving adults to draw near in order to remove the aloneness and temper the sense of disconnection.

When Their Friends Reject Them

Chris stood up for what he believed, and it may have cost him a friendship. On Friday night, Chris went cruising with Tony and

Gil in Tony's car. When Tony saw his brother's college roommate in front of the liquor store, he swerved into the parking lot.

"Hey, Spanky," Tony called. "Do me a favor."

Chris knew immediately what was going on. Tony was going to persuade Spanky to buy some beer for them. They were under-age, but Spanky wasn't.

"Guys, I can't go along with this," Chris protested. "Let's do something else."

"Oh, that's right, I forgot," Tony said. "You don't do this sort of thing." Chris detected a sarcastic note in his friend's voice. "Look," Tony said, facing Chris. "We won't open it, okay? I'll just save it for another time, when you're not with us."

Chris didn't want to start anything with his friends, but he didn't feel right about what they were doing, and he tried to dissuade them from it. But when Tony saw that Spanky was getting impatient, he gave him the money and told him, "Go ahead. We'll work this out."

"Tell you what," Chris said when he saw Spanky go into the store. "I'll get home myself, okay?" He opened the car door. "I'll see you guys later." As Chris walked away from the car, he grimaced at the angry words Tony hurled at his back. Gil didn't say anything, but Chris knew he would never cross Tony.

Chris had no idea whether Tony and Gil would stay mad at him. He knew he should be proud of himself for standing up to them. But all he felt was lonely right then. Being rejected and ridiculed by your friends is a stiff price to pay for doing the right thing.

As Chris discovered, the pressures to conform to a godless culture can produce a painful disconnection when kids don't go along with the crowd and are rejected for it.

When Families Split Up

A great loss occurs in the life of a young person when his or her parents divorce and Mom or Dad moves out. For example, if a student has a close relationship with his or her father—and suddenly Dad is only available on weekends—he or she may go through some very lonely times.

"I used to be close to my dad," Sandi says, "but now I hardly ever see him. He always used to understand my problems and always said just the right thing. But who am I going to talk to now? We talk when we see each other, but it's not like it used to be."

The loss of divorce brings many changes in a family, and most of them are unpleasant for the young people involved. Adding to the pain, students hesitate to share their loneliness with their parents, knowing that Mom and Dad already have enough problems. So the youth's sense of isolation and disconnection increases at a time when he or she desperately needs a friend and confidant.

If you know a young person suffering through this situation, you might want to consider offering them the small book *My Friend Is Struggling with Divorce of Parents* from the Friendship 911 collection (see Appendix A). Read the book first, then give it to the student. After he or she reads the book, offer to meet with him or her to discuss it and to be a source of comfort, support, and encouragement to that young person.

When a Romance Ends

A devastating sense of aloneness and loss often occurs when a close dating relationship between two students ends. The hurt is most intense when one student calls off the relationship while the other is still interested in staying together. The spurned individual feels hurt, unloved, and disconnected. Young people may imagine that they will never love no one else or that no one else will ever love them.

Young students don't always know what is best for them. It is sometimes painful for them to give up what they think they want but cannot have. God has better things in mind for them. He knows them better than they know themselves, and He always wants them to have His best. Even when students understand this truth, they still hurt like crazy when love leaves. We may not be able to answer all their "why" questions, but we can help ease the pain of separation.

When Friends or Family Members Die

Sara knew she had to go see her mother, but she hesitated at the idea. To Sara, walking through those doors meant that her mother was really in that sterile room connected to all those machines, and she did not want to admit that. Horrible accidents occurred in other people's lives, not in hers. Moments later, Sara was walking down a dimly lit hall toward the intensive care unit. Pastor O'Neill and Sara's father walked ahead.

When Sara first glimpsed the patient on the bed, she was relieved. It was not her mother. At least it did not look like her mother. The woman's puffy face was a collage of dark blue, purple, crimson, and pasty white. Her head was swathed in a bandage from the surgery. Tubes protruding from the mouth and nose further distorted her face. And the sparkling green eyes that Sara loved were covered by swollen, bluish-purple lids. Sara moved closer to confirm the faint hope that this was someone else's mother, not hers.

But her father's reaction told Sara that she was mistaken. He slipped his hand around his wife's pale, limp hand on the sheet and began talking to her softly, lovingly. After a minute, it was Sara's turn. She moved to the bed to stand beside her father.

Gazing upon the still form, Sara could finally see a resemblance to her mother. The shock of hair sticking out of the bandage was her mother's color. The shape of the ear and dimpled chin were also familiar. *I don't want it to be you, Mom, but it* is *you,* she admitted silently.

At this moment there were no tears. Another strong emotion was boiling up inside her as she gazed upon the near-lifeless body. Sara clenched her jaw to keep the sudden, angry words from blurting out of her mouth: *God, why did You let this happen to my mother?*

A few days later, Sara's mother died. The sadness of the moment seemed unbearable. She also felt occasional flashes of anger at the circumstances that had taken her mother away. And there were stabs of fear as she considered the days ahead without her mother's friendship and counsel.[1]

Perhaps the greatest inner pain any student can ever feel is caused by the death of a family member or close friend. You may have lost someone you loved dearly: a parent, a child, a spouse, or a close friend. You know the emptiness, the deep ache, and the loneliness you have felt for that person. You know the grief that you carried and may still carry. Young people who lose someone dear feel that grief intensely. Even when they have a supportive, loving family and caring friends who will walk through the experience with them, the ordeal can be very difficult. But without the loving involvement of a caring adult, the burden can seem unbearable. Grieving students need to connect with someone in this time of pain.

Years ago, a person shared with my wife the "three 'Be's'" of comforting someone who is experiencing the loss of a loved one: (1) be there, (2) be sensitive, and (3) be quiet. Comforting those in need isn't so much about saying all the right things as it is about knowing how to be there with them emotionally.

The small book *My Friend Is Struggling with the Loss of a Loved One* from the Friendship 911 collection will be of great help as you seek to comfort a grieving student.

CONNECTING THROUGH COMFORT

As with young people suffering disappointment over a sad event, kids who are suffering a relational loss need comfort. This is your starting point for entering a student's world. Kids need to sense your warmth and compassion as they go through the loss of relational separation.

When I was a young Christian, I thought that the Lord was too perfect to associate with our human feelings. For years I felt that He was a stainless-steel God—radiant, pure, and invincible but without feelings. But as I read the Bible and got to know Jesus for myself, I made a startling discovery. I found out that Jesus has feelings. Not only that, I saw that He has feelings for *me!* I found, with great delight, that a favorite word to describe Jesus when He was on earth was *compassion*. Over and over again I noticed the Bible saying that Jesus had compassion for hurting, lonely, and disconnected people. His love is not some impersonal, abstract, emotionless force; on the contrary, Jesus is warm, tender, gentle, kind, and sensitive.

> Kids who are suffering a relational loss need comfort.

Young people who are hurting because of relational separation or loss need comfort from the compassionate Christ. Through prayer and God's Word, young people can receive great comfort. But as we have indicated again and again in this book, God is also pleased to share some of His compassion and comfort to hurting young people through others. I believe God wants to use you to provide the comfort your hurting students need. During times of grief, comfort your kids with the comfort you received from God when you were hurting.

As Paul wrote in 2 Corinthians 1:4, we are to "comfort those in any trouble with the comfort we ourselves have received from God." "But Josh," you may say, "what if I don't feel compassionate at that moment toward a student who is hurting?" If you don't sense compassion for a hurting student, ask God to share His compassion with you. Pray something like this: "God, You are a compassionate God, and I know You are touched by the pain and loneliness this student feels in his relational loss. Share Your compassion with me so I can share it with my young friend." You will be surprised at how God's compassion will touch your heart in response to your request.

The words you speak—and don't speak—are critical to the ministry of sharing comfort with kids suffering relational loss. Initially, let your words be few. Resist the temptation to offer glib, spiritual-sounding platitudes or even well-intended Bible verses. It's better to be silently supportive at first than to spout clichés.

When you do speak, focus on simply feeling with the hurting student. Say things like, "I'm sorry"; "I know it hurts"; "I hurt for you"; "I wish you didn't have to feel this pain." Avoid saying, "God must need her more than you do"; "It must have been His will that your friend move away"; "Be thankful that you had your close friend as long as you did"; "At least he's not in pain anymore."

Help the young person let out the sorrow and pain he or she is feeling. Encourage him or her to express grief, even through tears. Be ready to say, "Go ahead and let it out"; "I know it hurts"; "I'm so sorry"; "I'm here for you"; "I'm going to help you get through this." Avoid saying: "Keep your chin up"; "Try to be strong"; "Dry up those tears and put on a happy face"; "Look on the bright side"; "Everything will be all right" (it may not be for quite a while).

Remember that a hurting, grieving student will seldom be helped by correction, instruction, or admonition. The best thing you can do to impart hope into the painful situation is to offer assurance of your continued presence and comfort.

What Else Can Be Done During Times of Relational Loss?

Comfort is perhaps the greatest need a young person has during times of relational loss. But there are at least two other things you can provide to a young person who feels the pain of a relational loss. The first is to provide encouragement. A suddenly ended relationship may dull a young person's focus on his or her goals in life, especially if the lost individual—a serious boyfriend or girlfriend, a parent, or another close relative—has been a significant influence in that young person's life. After sharing your comfort, you can encourage your young person with specifics on how he or she can adapt to his or her life and help with plans to begin to accommodate the loss that has been suffered.

Another important thing you can provide a young person during this time of pain is loving support. Whether separation occurs through rejection by friends, a geographical move, parental divorce, a breakup, or a death, a large void is left in the life of the student. You can help keep that student connected by entering his or her world with supportive efforts to help fill the void. If the student has lost a friend, what can you do to get him involved with other students so new friendships can begin? If the student has been separated from a parent through divorce, he or she may need to find a compassionate, mature parent figure, an adult to whom he or she can

> You can help keep that student connected by entering his or her world with supportive efforts to help fill the void.

relate. How can you find such a person and get the two together? Whatever the loss, perhaps you can fill the void by offering to take a more active role in the student's life for a time.

Great losses, such as the breakup of a romance or the death of a loved one, are obvious hurts for a young person, and you should respond accordingly. But a student's day-to-day life can be sprinkled with minor relational losses, such as a friend's rejection, a teacher's criticism, etc. These hurts may be more difficult to spot and minister to. But as you remain committed to entering your young person's world, noticing how he or she may be suffering, and making the appropriate connecting points, the emotional attachment between the two of you will only grow deeper.

CHAPTER 11

Connecting in Their World of Conflicts

Remember Ken Meyers from chapter 2? Ken is the fifteen-year-old who was doing his homework when his dad came in and gave him a lot of grief about his study habits and grades. Ken's dad and mom always seemed to be criticizing him about something: his music, his clothes, his hair, or his friends. The frequent conflicts at home caused him to lift this silent prayer: *God, why are Dad and Mom so against me? Why don't they care about me anymore? I know some things I do really tick them off. But they seem to hate everything about me. It's like they are tired of being my parents and would just rather I would grow up and move out. God, what can I do?*

Do you know a young person like Ken who struggles with relationships with his or her parents? Do your own kids seem at times to be at odds with you? Would the young people in your life say they feel criticized more than complimented? If so, these young people feel the strain of conflicts. (See pg. 231 for more information on the small book *My Friend Is Struggling with Conflicts with Others.*)

In many respects, conflicts in life are unavoidable. No parent, youth worker, or Christian educator is able to perfectly make the

165

relational connecting points with their students every single time. And even if they did, there is no 100-percent guarantee that a conflict can always be resolved by meeting one or more of a young person's relational needs. But we can say that by entering a young person's world with the intent of connecting relationally, you will succeed in resolving the conflict far more often than not.

CONNECTING IN THE CONFLICT

I believe many adult/child conflicts fester into a severe relational disconnection because the adult backs off emotionally during disagreements or relational friction and ceases to express affirmation, acceptance, appreciation, and affection to their kids. Yet during those times of differences, young people need their parents and caring adults to make those relational connecting points perhaps more than at any other time.

To help you know better how to enter your students' world of conflict and make that relational connection, consider these two things. First, learn to identify the specific needs your young people have behind their deeds. Try to understand what they are really reaching out for. Second, let your kids know you are doing your best to enter their world to connect with them where they need it and when they need it.

IDENTIFYING THE NEEDS BEHIND THEIR DEEDS

It is important to learn what your young person needs at the time he or she needs it. Showing appreciation to a young person who needs comfort misses the mark. Ken Meyers needed to know that his dad accepted him, but his dad only saw a need for accountability. Learn to identify the relational needs behind your kids' deeds. The following list of statements under each connecting point can help you identify relational needs by observing a young person's attitudes and behavior.

Affirmation

Your students feel affirmed when you identify with what they are feeling. When they don't feel affirmed by you, they may express the following in word or attitude:

- My parents just don't understand me.

- We're so different.

- I feel like my youth minister doesn't care what happens to me.

- My teacher doesn't think what I feel or think is very important.

Acceptance

Your students' need for acceptance is met when you let them know you love them for who they are, regardless of what they do. These statements reflect a student who isn't feeling accepted:

- I wish my parents would love me for who I am, not who they want me to be.

- I feel like my parents don't think I'm a very good person.

- It seems that my youth minister criticizes me all the time.

- My Sunday-school teacher sometimes makes me feel like a complete failure.

Appreciation

Your kids feel appreciated when you share words of gratitude or praise for what they do. If you suspect that they might agree with any of these statements, you probably aren't connecting with them:

- My parents seldom notice when I do something around the house.

- Mom and Dad talk about my bad behavior but hardly ever mention the good things.

- I don't think my teacher is even aware of my positive qualities.

- I hardly ever hear "Thank you" from my youth leader.

Affection

Affection is communicated through physical closeness and loving words. A lack of adult/student affection is reflected in the following statements:

- It seems that my parents treat my brother and sister better than they treat me.

- My parents hardly ever tell me they love me.

- Dad and Mom seldom hug me or kiss me anymore.

- I know my youth leader cares about me, but sometimes he doesn't act like it.

Availability

Your young people's need for time is met when you enter their world by showing interest and concern for who they are and what they do. If you suspect that one or more of the following statements are true of your youth, perhaps their need for your involvement in their life is not being fully met:

- My parents don't really listen to me.
- My youth leader doesn't have time for me.
- Dad and Mom rarely do anything with me.
- My youth leader almost never comes to anything I'm involved in (concerts, ball games, etc.).

Accountability

Young people want boundaries in order to feel safe. When there is little structured accountability, a young person may express these thoughts and feelings:

- My parents don't really care what I do.
- Mom and Dad have their lives, and I have mine.
- I wish my youth leader would care more about what I do.
- It's hard for me to admit, but I do need my parents to love me.

LETTING THEM KNOW YOU'RE TRYING

Failing to make a relational connection with your young person during or immediately following a disagreement may contribute to further conflicts. But when your child knows you are trying the best you can, it will make all the difference in the world. In fact, I have personally gone so far as to ask my kids to hold me accountable to connecting to them. For example, when Kelly's seventh birthday rolled around, I put a special note from me in her birthday card:

Dear Kelly,

I sure love you. I count it such a joy to be your dad, but you know, I'm going to need your help this year. I've never been the father of a seven-year-old daughter before. I just want to be the best dad I can be to you. And if you ever feel that I'm not doing right or not being fair, or loving and considerate, please tell me.

My birthday-card message to Kelly gave me the courage to open up and share that I wanted to be a good parent and that I needed her help. Kids don't require us to be perfect—just honest, open, and willing to admit our weaknesses. Here are some steps that can help you keep the connection even during conflicts.

Schedule a Time to Share

Find a suitable time when you and your young person can spend some time together without being interrupted. Your get-together should be timed to take place when the air between you is reasonably free of current unresolved issues. You may want to take him or her out to dinner or for ice cream. Perhaps a drive in the country or a hike would provide a healthy atmosphere for your discussion. Then share your heart. Let the student know you want to be there for him or her. Ask him or her to help you by letting you know when you've blown it and how you can stay better connected.

Prepare Prayerfully

Ask God to give you a pure heart and a good attitude for sharing, and ask the same for your student. Ask God to help you express your thoughts and concerns lovingly and in ways your young person will understand and readily respond to. You may want to write out what you want to say so you can read it to your student. A "Relational Connecting Interview" is provided in this chapter to guide interaction with your student.

Express Your Love

Begin the conversation by verbalizing your care and commitment to your child. Focus on the positive aspects of your relationship. Mention as many positive things as you can about your relationship and convey your genuine gratitude. You might find it meaningful to share something similar to the message I gave to Kelly in her birthday card.

Invite a Response

Say something like, "I want our relationship to grow stronger and deeper, and I am committed to doing everything I can for that to happen. I want to make sure that we are connected and stay connected. Would it be all right if I ask you several questions that will help me learn how to be the best parent (or youth leader) I can be?"

Use some or all of the following questions to facilitate your time together and help you express how you might better connect with your student. These questions are designed to elicit his or her thoughts or concerns about the need for your affirmation, acceptance, appreciation, affection, availability, and accountability. With each question, be ready to ask for examples to draw out your student's deepest thoughts and feelings on the subject. Also be ready to ask, "How can I be more sensitive to you in this area?" Take careful note of your young person's answers. They will reveal areas in which you can better understand him or her and keep conflicts between you from causing a major relational disconnection.

RELATIONAL CONNECTING INTERVIEW

Affirmation
1. Do you sense that I want to understand the things you're going through?
2. Do you feel that I'm excited about the things that excite you?
3. Do you sense that I feel sad for you when you're disappointed or have had a rough day?
4. Do you really feel free to share how you feel with me?

Acceptance
1. Do you feel that I accept you for exactly who you are?
2. When I point out an area that needs improvement, do you feel as if I'm personally disapproving of you?
3. Are there times when I make you feel like a failure?

Appreciation
1. Does it sometimes seem I don't notice when you do something helpful?
2. Do I talk to you more about what you don't do right than about the good things you do?

3. Do you sometimes wonder if I am aware of your positive qualities?

4. Do I often fail to say thank you when you need to hear it?

Affection

1. Do you often feel as though I treat your brother or sister (or other students) better than I treat you?

2. Do you feel that I rarely ever tell you that I love (or care about) you?

3. (Parents only) Do you feel that I hardly ever hug you or kiss you anymore?

Availability

1. Do you sometimes feel that I don't really listen to you?

2. Do you sometimes feel that I don't have much time for you?

3. Do you wish that I would do more things with you?

4. Do you wish that I would be more involved in your activities (concerts, performances, ball games, etc.)? If so, how would you like me to be involved?

Accountability

1. Do you feel as if I lay down too many family rules for you?

2. Do you think I give you the rules because I don't trust you?

3. Do you believe I restrict you or set rules because I love (or care about) you?

4. (Parents only) How could I give you future guidance and input so that it reinforces to you that I really want to provide for you and protect you?

The more open and responsive you are to your young person's answers, the more he or she will open up honestly to you. You may hear things that are uncomfortable to hear. But in the long run, this time together can help you to know better how to enter your students' world not only to connect, but to stay connected.

CHAPTER 12

Connecting in Their World of Love and Sex

After the planetarium show, Luke and Traci, high-school juniors, strolled to a bench outside where they could see the city lights. Luke draped his jacket around Traci's shoulders and wrapped her in his arms. Alone on the bench, huddled with Traci to stay warm, Luke's desire for her heated up. Her willingness spurring him on, Luke's kisses became more passionate than ever before in their two-month relationship. The moment was intense, and he just wanted to be closer to her. Traci's response told him she wanted the same thing.

Once they returned to the car and resumed their romantic huddling, Luke could hardly keep himself under control. His feelings for Traci were so strong, not like anything he had felt for other girls. It was a hunger that just seemed to grow more intense with every date. It took all the willpower he could muster to stop before it was too late. "We had better get home," he said, pulling away from her reluctantly.

"Yeah, I guess so," Traci said timidly.

They drove home in silence. Luke felt embarrassed for being

so bold in his physical approach to Traci, but he seemed almost driven. Why did he feel more strongly toward Traci than any other girl he had dated? Why did he feel so physically and sexually attracted to her? As the car wound down the hill toward the city, the thought occurred to him for the first time: *My desire for Traci is so strong because I must be in love with her.*

Meanwhile, Traci was ashamed of her behavior, seemingly on the verge of breaking her vow of purity to God. *Forgive me, God, for compromising my standards,* she prayed silently as Luke drove her home. Traci had been swept away by her emotions tonight. The romantic dinner, the candles, the stars, Luke's eagerness to make her feel special—everything was so right. He had been so sweet and affectionate to her, she would have done anything to please him. She hoped this would not be their last time together, because she did not want to lose this great guy.[1]

Young People Are Getting Mixed Signals

The culture's distorted view of love and sex sends confusing and mixed signals to our kids of what true love is and is not. Too often kids like Luke and Traci confuse the intensity of sex with the intimacy of love.

If there is any area in which our young people need their parents, youth workers, and Christian educators, it is the area of guiding them through the biblical perspective of love and sex. They need you to enter their world of love and sex, to stay relationally connected to them, and to give them sound, practical, God-centered insight.

Today our kids need to know: "What is true love?"; "Am I in love right now?"; "Will I know it when I am?"; "When I really love someone, is it okay to have sex?" These are major questions in the minds of young people like Traci and Luke. Many kids grapple with these delicate, emotionally charged issues alone because the significant adults in their lives are either unwilling or unavailable to talk about them. When you enter a young person's world to strengthen a loving bond with him or her, you need to be prepared to deal with these questions—even if they are not asked directly.

Everybody, no matter what age, wants and needs true love. Without love, life would be incomplete at best, desperate at worst. The yearning to give and receive love throbs in the heart of male and female alike. People try in many different ways to discover a love that is real, a love that lasts for all time. Yet the pursuit of love has caused more heartache, pain, brokenness, and bitterness than all the diseases and wars in human history.

> Many young people struggle to understand what love is and how they can find it.

Many young people struggle to understand what love is and how they can find it. Many are willing to give almost anything to experience love, particularly from someone of the opposite sex. To many kids, love really *does* make the world go round. Yet so many set themselves up for heartache, disappointment, and tragic mistakes because they lack a clear understanding of what love is—and what it isn't. (For more information on the small book *My Friend Is Struggling with Knowing True Love*, see Appendix A.)

What True Love Is Not

One of the most important ways to stay connected with your young people as they struggle through thoughts and feelings about love is to be there with open and honest answers to their questions. And one of the most often asked questions is, "What is true love?" The first step to identifying true love is to help kids see what true love *is not*.

True Love Is Not the Same as Lust

Love and lust are often confused in our culture. In fact, many of today's movies, popular songs, and novels about love are really about lust. How can you tell the difference? Love gives; lust takes. Love values; lust uses. Love endures; lust subsides. Luke may be a little confused between the two. He enjoys being close to Traci because she awakens his pleasurable sexual urges and feelings. He does nice things for Traci at least in part because she is more willing to share the physical closeness and intimacy that he enjoys. And his lust nearly caused him to compromise his sexual purity and hers.

God designed us with the desire and capacity for sexual intimacy. But if a student's interaction with someone of the opposite sex is based on intense sexual feelings and physical gratification, lust may be playing the role of love in the relationship.

True Love is Not the Same as Romance

When Luke and Traci were together, they could almost hear violins playing sweet love music. When they kissed, emotional fireworks went off inside. Whenever Luke spoke sweet words of love and affection or cared for Traci in kind, romantic ways, she felt like a princess. Whenever Traci gazed lovingly into his eyes, Luke felt stronger and more important than anyone else. Candlelight dinners, soft music, and starry skies brought on intense romantic feelings in both of them, especially Traci.

Romantic feelings are wonderful in a close male/female relationship. God wired us to experience these feelings with the opposite sex.

> Romance is a feeling;
> true love is much more.

Perhaps your young person has enjoyed the inner warmth and fireworks of romance in a dating relationship. But the excitement and warmth of romance cannot be equated to love. Romance is a feeling; true love is much more.

True love Is Not the Same as Infatuation

Infatuation is a fascination with and intense interest in someone of the opposite sex. He thinks about her all day and dreams about her at night. She plans her day around seeing or talking to him. Her thoughts and his thoughts may be so preoccupied with each other that neither one of them can concentrate on anything else. Another term for infatuation is *puppy love*. Puppy love may be real to a puppy, but if the only love your young person experiences is puppy love, he or she will end up living a dog's life!

When people talk about "falling in love" or "love at first sight," they are usually talking about infatuation. Infatuation left Traci feeling breathless and starry-eyed about Luke. And Luke sometimes felt lightheaded and

> Infatuation is not
> wrong, but it should not be
> mistaken for love.

addlebrained being with Traci. Maybe your student has experienced similar feelings about someone of the opposite sex. Infatuation is not wrong, but it should not be mistaken for love.

True Love Is Not the Same as Sex

Many students (and many adults as well) confuse the intensity of sexual desire with true love. It happened to Luke after his sexual hunger for Traci nearly caused him to abandon his promise to remain sexually pure. His strong desire to experience sex with her caused him to wonder if his feelings were based on true love. Perhaps the young people in your life have wondered the same thing about their sexual desires.

Sex as God intended it is not wrong. It was designed by God for procreation and fulfillment within the bounds of marriage. But sex and love are distinct. You can have sex without love and love without sex. Love is a process; sex is an act. Love is learned; sex is instinctive. Love requires constant attention; sex takes no ongoing effort. Love takes time to develop and mature; sex needs no time to develop. Love requires emotional and spiritual interaction; sex requires only physical interaction. Love deepens a relationship; sex without love dulls a relationship.

"If love is more than lust, romance, infatuation, or sex," the young person may ask, "how do I know if I'm in love?" That's the big question, especially when he or she is attracted to members of the opposite sex and increasingly involved in dating. To answer that question, you need to help kids know more than what true love *isn't*. They need to understand what true love *is*.

WHAT TRUE LOVE IS

Just as many people confuse love with lust, romance, infatuation, and sex, many are also in the dark about the different kinds of love people express. There are basically three ways of behaving in relationships that people routinely label as "love." You will help your kids clear up the mixed signals about what true love is when you help them understand the differences.

"I love you if . . ."

If love is conditional love. It is given or received only when certain conditions are met. The only way to get this kind of love is to earn it by performing in an approved manner. Some parents love their children *if* they behave well, *if* they get good grades, or *if* they act or dress a certain way. Among married or dating couples, love may be withheld *if* one partner fails to do or be what the other wants. *If* love is basically selfish. It is a bargaining chip offered in exchange for something desired.

Many young women have only experienced the kind of love that says, "I love you *if* you give me what I want sexually" or "I love you *if* you have sex with me just this once." Another subtle sexual *if* pressure is found in the common misconception that all dating couples are having sex. The message is, "Since everyone is doing it, you will love me if you do it too." What these girls don't realize is that the love they expect to win from a boy by meeting his sexual demands is only a cheap imitation of love intended to compromise a girl's character. It cannot satisfy the need for love, and it is never worth the price of sexual compromise.

If love always has strings attached. As long as certain conditions prevail, the relationship is fine. But when expectations are not met, *if* love is withdrawn. Many marriages break up because they were built on *if* love. When one or both partners fail to perform to the desired standard, "love" turns to disappointment and resentment.

Luke's "love" for Traci at this point may be largely based on *if* love. As long as Traci makes him feel good, as long as she dresses to please him, as long as she allows him to enjoy her closeness, he is interested in her. But what would happen to Luke's "love" if Traci said, "No more kissing, no more handholding, and certainly no more intense cuddling in the car"? Would he still want to be with her and spend his hard-earned money to show her a good time?

If love is not true love. If a young person is in a relationship in which he or she senses pressure to perform in a certain way to gain the love he or she desires, the relationship is not governed by true love.

"I love you because . . ."

The second kind of love, *because* love, is a close cousin to *if* love. One person loves another because of something he or she is, has, or does. Someone may say, "I love you *because* you are so beautiful" or "I love you *because* you take good care of me" or "I love you *because* you make me laugh." Traci may be an example of *because* love, since she is strongly attracted to Luke because he is so sweet, kind, and romantic around her.

Because love sounds pretty good. Almost everyone appreciates being loved for who they are or what they do. It is certainly preferable to *if* love, which must be constantly earned and requires a lot of effort. Being loved because we are good-looking, witty, kind, wealthy, popular, etc., seems much less demanding and conditional than trying to bargain for love.

But what will happen to Traci's love when she meets someone who is sweeter and kinder than Luke? How will she treat him when he is no longer an impressive youth-group leader or if he cannot afford to take her on romantic dates? If Traci's love is based on who Luke is and what he does, it may not survive any negative changes in his role or performance.

Because love is not true love. A student may be attracted to someone because of his or her personality, position, intelligence, skill, popularity, or ability. But if the student's love is not founded on more than what the other person is, has, or does, it will not last.

"I love you, period."

The third kind of love is love without conditions. This kind of love says, "I love you despite what you may be like deep down inside. I love you no matter what might change about you. You can't do anything to turn off my love." True love is a love that loves, period!

Love, period is not blind. It can and should know a great deal about the other person. It may be aware of that person's failures, shortcomings, and faults. Yet it totally accepts that person without demanding anything in return. There is no way you can earn this type of love, nor can you lose it. It has no strings attached.

Love, period is different from *if* love in that it does not require certain conditions to be met before it is given. It is also different from *because* love in that it is not generated by attractive or desirable qualities in the other person. Lust, romance, infatuation, sex, *if* love, and *because* love are predominantly about getting something from another person. True love is about giving to another person. Luke and Traci are still closer to the getting side in their relationship. If what they identify as love is to grow into true love, each of them will need to make a transition to the giving side.

THIS CRAZY THING CALLED LOVE

Here are a few practical ways you can help your kids as they try to figure out "this crazy thing called love." They all involve entering their world and teaching them with care and compassion about the real meaning of love.

Take your student on a one-on-one "date" or to a place he or she enjoys.

Use your time away to talk to your student about what love is and what love isn't. Share the information as a friend without probing into his or her love life or condemning for any past mistakes. You might want to use the small book *My Friend Is Struggling with Knowing True Love*. Invite questions and encourage him or her to share thoughts on the subject. Make this discussion an annual event.

Occasionally talk about your own experiences of discovering the difference between true love and its many counterfeits.

You may even want to discreetly admit your own mistakes and misconceptions. It will help the youth realize that he or she is not the only one who sometimes learns about love by trial and error.

Write a letter or series of letters to the student, explaining what love is.

Also include in your letters what love isn't, including your own experiences.

Use TV programs, movies, and popular music as discussion starters on the topic of true love.

As you watch or listen with the student, ask questions like, "What kind of love is being presented here? How can you tell? What would true love look like in this situation?"

DATING IS A BIG DEAL

"Why is it such a big thing," one girl asks, "if I don't have a date every Friday night?"

"I know I probably shouldn't feel this way," echoes another student, "but I can't help thinking that if I'm not dating, I'm a zero."

"Why can't I be satisfied with having friends?" questions another youth. "My friends are important to me, but I really, really want to be special to someone."

These are fair questions, ones that every young person must deal with. Dating, being accepted, being liked, and being "special" to at least one member of the opposite sex is a big deal to most kids. And yet many of the adults in their lives minimize or ignore these first expeditions into the uncharted jungles of youthful love. Kids hear statements like, "You can't be in love; you're too young"; "It's nothing more than puppy love"; "Quit daydreaming about dating and get your homework done"; "There are plenty more fish in the sea, so just get over it."

Why are dating and thoughts of love such a big deal to kids? There are several reasons.

Young people are going through several physical changes that heighten their sense of sexuality.

Socially and emotionally, these changes become associated with being attractive or desirable. Girls are beginning to look more like women. Guys are growing taller and stronger, filling out a man-sized frame. This transformation causes a kid to realize, "Hey, something is happening to me; I'm growing up."

Dating is a tangible way to find out if someone else notices that he or she is an attractive, desirable person. This is not to say that dating is solely based on physical appearance. But in our looks-conscious society, it is certainly a contributing factor to most kids. The challenge is to help kids keep physical attraction from being the basis for social relationships.

Once I heard a woman in her mid-twenties comment about her early teen years. "In junior high," she said, "I thought I was popular with the guys. Now I think it was because I was the only thin girl in our youth group—all of the other girls were fat!" Perhaps her "popularity" had more to do with genetic and biological luck—and with the narrow dating views of her schoolmates—than personality. Dating experiences, for better or worse, influence whether or not young people feel okay about their physical and social development.

> Dating experiences, for better or worse, influence whether or not young people feel okay about their physical and social development.

Dating often seems like an approval rating on a student's personality.

Our culture consistently links desirability to dating. Advertising and television programs play a lot on this theme. The girl who dresses right, has her hair fixed properly, drinks the right soft drink, and uses the right tanning lotion is popular with the guys. When kids approach such ideas rationally, they know they are not true. But kids don't usually live by logic. Their emotions tell them that they want to do all the things— superficial as they may be—that TV and movies and commercials tell them will make them popular to their friends and their peer group.

*Dating is a big deal to kids because of the social
expectations that others place on them.*

Most students don't want to be left out when their peers are
filling up their weekends with dates. Friends drop little hints that
increase the pressure: "What are *you* doing Friday night?";
"Who are you attending the prom with?"; "What did you do last
weekend?" Sometimes parents add to the pressure by nudging
their young people into dating relationships so they are not considered social outcasts. And what about the youth leader who
innocently asks, "Who is the special person in your life?" or pro-
motes activities that especially cater to couples? These pressures
may make students feel worse about not having a special someone in their lives.

*Dating is important because many young people are
hungry for the affection that comes from being special
to someone.*

Obviously, this has both healthy and unhealthy potential.
In God's original design, He intended that children receive significant doses of love and affection from their parents. Dads
are especially important to supplying this need. Sadly, many
dads are unavailable to their kids either because of work,
divorce, or other activities or because they feel uncomfortable
giving warm, positive affection to their kids. Thus, many children arrive at adolescence feeling a powerful need to be cher-
ished by someone else.

Dating often helps to meet this need for affection. But kids
with unmet emotional needs, particularly girls, are vulnerable to
sexual exploitation. Their hunger for affection easily breaks
down the moral barriers to sexual restraint.

Dating seems to meet a youth's need for intimacy.

God designed us with a valid need for intimate, fulfilling relationships. Even a young person longs to share himself or herself at a deep level with another person. That's what true intimacy is: sharing every part of your life with someone else. Every youth desires someone who will love and accept him or her for who he or she is, someone he or she can trust and open up to without fear of rejection. Kids have an inborn desire for love and intimacy, but most don't know how to find it.

> Kids have an inborn desire for love and intimacy, but most don't know how to find it.

Since kids are sometimes clueless about how to find the intimacy they seek, they may see dating, physical closeness, and even sex as the way to "instant intimacy." But instant intimacy—and I don't believe there is such a thing—creates an illusion of love that is no more than skin-deep, which ultimately leads to frustration, guilt, and greater loneliness.

Dating is important because young people have a healthy longing to connect socially with a person of the opposite sex.

Guys and girls are naturally curious about how the opposite sex thinks about life. The following comments are typical of the insights kids gain from each other by spending time with someone of the opposite sex.

"Can you believe," Mark confides to his best friend, "Shelly says that she and her girlfriends aren't always talking about, you know, what we talk about. She says they don't think as much about sex as we do. Do you think she's telling the truth?"

Shelly sits cross-legged on her bed across from her friend Pam. "Mark can be so funny sometimes," she says. "He always has to be doing something. If we go to the mall, he's got to play games in the arcade, stuff like that. It seems like he never just wants to sit and talk."

Dating can be a means for satisfying a healthy curiosity about, and interest in, the opposite sex.

Six Questions to Answer Before They Date

Where does dating fit into the life of your young person or the students you know? Some may feel lonely or left out because they do not date. Whether they date or not, they may be confused about where they stand with the opposite sex. Even those who date regularly may still feel lonely and wonder why. The dating dilemma, if not met with care by concerned adults, can lead to an emotional disconnection in students' lives.

> The dating dilemma, if not met with care by concerned adults, can lead to an emotional disconnection in students' lives.

Your loving interest and concern can help your students stay connected to you during their struggles and disappointments over dating. Kids need to be lovingly reminded about the real purposes of dating. In the midst of a culture that encourages kids to date for sex or prestige or attention or other forms of self-gratification, our Christian youth need to be lovingly pointed back to the biblical goals for relating to the opposite sex.

When you sense that a student is struggling with the concept of dating or has been discouraged by dating experiences, use the following questions to encourage him or her toward the right goals for dating:

"Are you keeping relationships in perspective?"

Sometimes an issue can get blown out of proportion and cause trouble. Are the student's dating troubles keeping him or her from seeing other positive things that are happening in his or her life? Remind the student that he has other good friends and loving parents. She is healthy and able to be involved in many activities she enjoys. And above all, Jesus loves him and is a constant companion.

"Are you turning down other relationship opportunities?"

What occasions for friendship has your student overlooked because he or she is too focused on dating? Could she get involved in student government or sports or clubs at school? Could he join a choir or do volunteer work in a service agency? Could she initiate "group dates" in which several students of both sexes get together for games and fun without "pairing off"?

"Do you need to work on your social skills?"

One female student, working at a Christian camp for the summer, shared a room with a female worker. This worker rarely took showers or washed her clothes. In fact, she had such poor hygiene that others avoided her. She not only missed out on dates with staff guys, she was often shunned by the other women at camp. Finally, the staff counselor asked the student's roommate to talk with the other girl about the problem. She needed someone to clue her in on some basic social skills.

While the above example is extreme, it does point out a common problem among young people: Many of them lack strong social skills. They need to realize that their peers will seldom come to them to talk about why others don't like being around them. Take the initiative to go to the student and lovingly but honestly talk about any offensive habits or personality quirks you have observed.

"Why are dating relationships so important to you?"

Has dating become a mark that the student is "okay"? Does he see that everyone else is doing it and feel that he must do it, too, to feel good about himself? Does she feel pressure from others to date? At times, students may become obsessed with the thought that they are abnormal if they're not doing what everyone else is doing. You may need to remind them that dating is not essential to happiness.

"Do you have realistic expectations?"

Unrealistic expectations in dating can lead to frustration, disappointment, and loneliness. Alex and Jan had been friends for a couple of years. When they were together with others in their youth group they had lots of fun. Then one day Alex's older brother suggested that Alex ask Jan for a date. They could double-date. Jan accepted.

The date turned out to be a complete failure. Whereas Alex and Jan had enjoyed a good friendship, Alex expected that Jan might want him to be "romantic" on the date. He tried to hold Jan's hand. She felt uncomfortable. He felt he ought to kiss her. Jan refused. The situation was tense because Alex had unrealistic expectations about being a "boyfriend," which involved being "romantic." Instead, he needed to continue being Jan's friend.

Encourage your student that it is okay to be friends with members of the opposite sex apart from any dating involvement.

"Are you nurturing your relationship with Jesus?"

Behind the idea of dating is the common desire to have a special relationship with someone. God wired your young people to need intimacy, affection, and transparency with another person. Kids need to be encouraged that close personal relationships begin with Jesus. I'm not being flippant when I say that Jesus has all the qualifications to be a perfect "date." He embodies everything a student needs in a special, intimate friend.

Jesus seeks young people's friendship. Revelation 3:20 is Christ's way of telling us that He wants a special relationship with every believer, a close and personal relationship.

Young people are special to Jesus. No one is common or ordinary to Jesus. No one is plain or unappealing to Him. Remind kids that, no matter what personality problems, physical flaws, or intellectual limitations they may see in themselves, Jesus likes them and loves them. No one can ever fill the place that Jesus has reserved for each one in His heart.

Jesus has affectionate feelings for every young person. When kids are upset, Jesus understands and cares. When something exciting happens and kids are pumped, Jesus is joyful with them. Because He is an affirming God, students can know that He shares their happiness and sadness. Frankly, it is probably a disappointment to Him when we don't include Him in the ups and downs of our lives. He is a kind, compassionate, understanding Lord who fully participates in all aspects of a student's life.

The topics of love and dating often become a tangled jumble of thoughts and emotions, leaving kids hurting and feeling alone. As you enter their world of young love, your insights will be a connecting bridge that will help them deal with the disappointments and misunderstandings of young love.

CHAPTER 13

Connecting in Their World of Sexual Pressure

Some time ago, a young lady poured her heart out to me in the following letter:

Dear Josh:

When I was only fourteen years of age, I dated an eighteen-year-old boy. After a month or so of dating, he told me that he loved me and had to "have me." He said that if I loved him, I would have sex with him. And if I wouldn't, he couldn't control his desire for me and would have to break up with me.

What did I think at fourteen years of age? I knew sex was wrong before marriage, yet I so desired to have a man love me. I was so insecure in my father's love and had a poor self-image. I always felt like I had to earn people's love. The better I was at home with my chores, the more As on my report card, the more my father loved me—or so it was communicated.

So here was my boyfriend, who I really liked (and thought I

193

loved), telling me he loved me. Well, I needed that love. . . . So I finally gave in.

I felt so guilty afterward. I can remember sobbing in my bed at night, after I'd come home from being with my boyfriend. I wanted so much to have my virginity back. My self-esteem certainly didn't improve, but worsened, and I needed my boyfriend's love more than ever. I began to feel so lonely inside, and yet there was no one I could turn to.

Well, after two years, I broke up with my boyfriend. But soon I had another boyfriend, and I went through the same cycle with him. And then with another. Was I any more secure with myself? No, I was a puppet in any man's hands, for I wanted so desperately to find someone who would love me unconditionally.

Isn't that ironic? The very thing I searched for—unconditional love—was being offered to me conditionally. "If you love me, you'll do it."

The saddest part about this story is that I have heard it—or something very similar to it—countless times from the kids I meet across the country and in the hundreds of letters they send to me. The pressure from peers and from the media for young people to be sexually active is staggering. Whether you realize it or not, your students feel it too. They need someone to enter their world and lovingly connect with them in the arena of sexual temptation and pressure.

> The pressure from peers and from the media for young people to be sexually active is staggering.

THE PRESSURE IS ON

Premarital sex is a significant problem in the disconnected generation. According to George Barna of the Barna Research Group, only 23 percent of post–baby boomers claim to be virgins. More than three-quarters admit to having had sexual intercourse with another single person. Two out of ten unmarried members of that generation say they have had sex with a married person, and of those who are

> Only 23 percent of post–baby boomers claim to be virgins.

married, one in fourteen have had extramarital sex. Almost half (47 percent) of the babies born to that generation in 1992 were born to unmarried mothers.[1] The *New York Times* reports, "Some studies indicate three-fourths of all girls have had sex during their teen-age years and 15 percent have had four or more partners."[2] And girls are having sex much earlier these days; the median age for a young woman's first act of premarital sex has fallen from nineteen in 1960 to seventeen in 1990.

Sexual activity among churched youth is likewise disturbing. By age eighteen, 27 percent have experienced sexual intercourse, and 55 percent of the young men have engaged in fondling breasts.

Research indicates that youth apparently become less—not more—resistant as they mature. From the youngest segment (eleven to twelve years old) to the next age category (thirteen to fourteen), the proportion of kids involved in heavy kissing doubles, the fondling of breasts increases fivefold, the fondling of genitals increases by a factor of seven, and the incidence of intercourse (experienced by 1 percent of the youngest age group) increases eight times (to one in eleven) through the course of the teen years.

Activity at each level of sexual involvement—fondling of breasts, fondling of genitals, and sexual intercourse—doubles among fifteen- to sixteen-year-olds (compared to those in the next youngest age group). By the age of sixteen, two in five (41 percent) have engaged in or permitted the fondling of breasts, nearly one in three (30 percent) have fondled genitals, and about one in five (18 percent) have taken part in sexual intercourse.

A majority are involved in heavy kissing and fondling of breasts by the time they reach the seventeen- to eighteen-year-old group. About two-thirds of the boys of that age have fondled breasts, an increase of 34 percent over the next youngest age group; nearly half of seventeen- and eighteen-year-old boys and girls have fondled the genitals of at least one other person, a 47-percent increase. And, due to the 50 percent rise in the incidence of intercourse among seventeen- to eighteen-year olds (compared to the next youngest age group), more than one in four (27 percent) admit to having gone "all the way."[3]

WHY KIDS SAY YES TO SEXUAL PRESSURE

The *New York Times* once observed that the typical high-school student "faces more sexual temptation on his way to school each morning than his grandfather did on Saturday night when he was out looking for it!"[4] Today's youth seem to be more aware of sex, more bombarded with sexually oriented messages, and more susceptible to the dangers of illicit sex than previous generations. Why? There are several reasons.

It Feels Good

God designed sexual intercourse to be pleasurable. A person who has premarital sex may feel guilt, remorse, shame, or even hatred toward the other person, but physically—and frequently relationally—premarital sex feels good. "Where I live," one student said, "many of my girl friends and guy friends are involved in sex because they just want to do it. When I ask them why, they usually say it makes them feel good."

> For many young people, sex is the drug that temporarily delivers them from emotional emptiness.

God has given each person a desire for intimacy, and we feel empty when that desire is not met. Developing relationships and true intimacy is sometimes difficult and always takes time. The easier and more predictable solution is to ease the pain artificially. Just as pills can deaden real physical pain, sensory experiences can temporarily deaden emotional pain. And for many young people, sex is the drug that temporarily delivers them from emotional emptiness. The letdown, the deepening pain, the fear, and the uncertainty will come later, but for now sex feels good.

Pressure from a Boyfriend or Girlfriend

The girl whose story opened this chapter felt this pressure, as many other young people do in dating relationships. It's a common line: "If you love me, you'll have sex with me." Some students get involved in sexual activity because they are afraid of losing a boyfriend or girlfriend. If a boy threatens to dump a girl because she won't give in, she may be fully aware that she is being manipulated. Yet if she has become dependent on him emotionally, she will do what he wants.

I've Done It Once, Why Not Again?

Students sometimes believe that once they have become sexually active, there is no use turning back. They feel they have already messed up, and there is no way to change the past. One girl felt that God could not use her because she was no longer a virgin, so she might as well have sex again. Christian young people who were sexually active before marriage and have fallen into this way of thinking often give up on God's forgiveness. But the beauty of God's forgiveness is that it never ends. We can come to Him in repentance any time, for any reason, no matter how long we have strayed from Him.

A Lack of Understanding About True Love

Biblical love gives without expecting anything in return, accepts without conditions, and provides security in a relationship apart from performance. Yet kids can grow up feeling insecure at home when they feel they must perform in order to earn their parents' love. Sometimes parents encourage this misconception by withholding love when a child misbehaves. As we pointed out in the previous chapter, kids who lack understanding about true love enter adolescence equating love with performance. This misunderstanding usually results in confusion about sex and love. Sex is an act performed by two people who are committed to loving each other for life, while love, in varying degrees, can be expressed by anyone apart from any sexual activity. Love is not an act; love is a commitment.

Peer Pressure

One boy says, "My three closest friends were all sexually active, or at least they said they were, from our sophomore year on. It seemed as if they always got the girls, even though all they would talk about was using them." Another comments, "My parents are always telling me what to do and what not to do about sex. I hate their nagging. Besides, everyone has done it. Nobody's a virgin." A girl adds, "The peer pressure from friends is probably the hardest to face as a virgin, because people will tease. 'It's fun; you're missing out. Are you chicken or something? It's great. You won't get pregnant.'"

Peer pressure as it operates among today's young people sometimes becomes a kind of moral blackmail. The basis for this blackmail is the group's power to accept or reject members. And in our permissive society, sexual activity is often seen as an important criterion for acceptance in a desired group. Even Christian kids, who have grown up with biblical morality, find themselves discarding or ignoring those values because of the fear of rejection.

Rebellion

Jessica liked to be around her friends because, when they were together, she didn't have to think about all the hurt her mom had caused her. One night, Jessica had a party at her house while her parents were away. She met Joe, a cute, intelligent guy, and she was immediately attracted to him. They talked a lot and got to know each other during the evening. Nearly everyone at the party paired off in different parts of the house. Jessica led Joe into her parents' bedroom, and they had sex that night in her parents' bed. It was the ultimate way for Jessica to rebel against her mother and the hurt she had caused.

Rebellion is one way students react when they feel disconnected from parents and other important adults in their lives.

Counselors say that a rebellious child is often reacting to poor relationships at home, both between parents and child and between the parents themselves. What better way to rebel in a strained relationship than to violate parental wishes or demands for sexual purity?

Curiosity

Kids see sex portrayed in the media as something glamorous, exhilarating, and exciting. They rarely see the negative emotional and physical consequences portrayed in the movies and on television programs. No wonder they ask themselves, *What does sex feel like? Is it really as great as they say?* Kids have a natural curiosity about the unknown. If the facts about sex are never discussed at home in a healthy manner, their curiosity about sex will only grow with time.

A Need for Security

If young people don't feel loved and secure in their relationships at home, they will seek that security elsewhere. One student explained the need for security:

> A girl's family is really having problems, and she needs someone to listen to her, care about her, and most of all love her. In her eyes, she needs someone who will just make her forget her problems, someone she can hold on to for security. She meets the "perfect guy," but this guy has basically the same problems and is looking for security as well. Neither one of them knows what real love is, and they may mistake it for sex. This is where a lot of people my age get into trouble.

People often use their bodies as buffers to avoid psychological intimacy. It is much easier to jump into bed and share our bodies with someone than it is to share our innermost thoughts. The excessive premarital and extramarital sex in our culture today are indicative of our inability to experience the security of true intimacy. The supposed security of a sexual encounter is a shallow substitute for the security and intimacy that come from a deep emotional connection.

THE PRICE OF YIELDING TO SEXUAL PRESSURE

The effects of yielding to sexual pressure fall into two general categories. First, there are the obvious physical consequences, all of which may complicate or endanger a student's life for years to come, such as the loss of virginity, an unplanned pregnancy, a "forced" marriage, or a sexually transmitted disease.

Beyond these tragic physical complications, however, are the devastating psychological and relational problems that often accompany or follow premarital sex. (See Appendix A for the small book *My Friend Is Struggling with an Unplanned Pregnancy.*)

Guilt

Like any form of immorality and disobedience from God's commands, nonmarital sex results in guilt. One woman testified, "I became sexually involved with my fiancé. We had convinced ourselves that sex outside of marriage was all right for us since we were engaged, but the Holy Spirit was convicting me that it was wrong. I felt incredibly guilty." In younger students, the guilt may seem even greater.

Emotional Distress

One girl explained the effects of her sexual involvement in these words:

> Having premarital sex was the most horrifying experience of my life. It wasn't at all the emotionally satisfying experience the world deceived me into believing it would be. I felt as if my insides were being exposed and my heart left unattended. . . . I know God has forgiven me of this haunting sin, but I also know I can never have my virginity back. I dread the day that I have to tell the man I truly love and wish to marry that he is not the only one, though I wish he were. . . . I have stained my life—a stain that will never come out.

Sexual immorality can breed suspicion, disappointment, sorrow, stress, emptiness, and many other destructive emotions.

Broken Relationships

In the words of one student, "Sex . . . hurt[s] a relationship, [and] it also makes it harder for a couple to break up." Premarital sex often makes participants feel trapped; it can hinder intimate conversation and trust; it can cause one or both participants to feel used; and, when a breakup occurs, it can be an emotionally ripping experience.

Self-Condemnation

Premarital sex can have a serious effect on the self-image of the person engaging in it. A poor self-concept, which is among the causes of premarital sexual involvement, is also among its results. Sexual involvement outside of marriage will often worsen a student's feelings of self-doubt, insecurity, humiliation, and self-loathing.

Sexual Addiction

Many students who become involved in premarital sexual intercourse come away from the experience with an intense desire for more. Trying to fill a spiritual vacuum with physical pleasure (which is impossible), sexually active students can become absorbed in their sexual pursuits. Curiosity and desire soon become the master, demanding to be satisfied yet never knowing fulfillment.

Spiritual Bondage

Sex is often the means by which our spiritual adversary (see 1 Pet. 5:8) binds young men and women spiritually and prods them into other risks and behaviors that endanger them physically, emotionally, and spiritually. Sexual involvement hinders a young person's walk with God, sometimes prompts a slackening of religious commitment, and traps him or her in a cycle of pressure and powerlessness. Furthermore, some studies have noted a relationship between premarital sex and other forms of delinquency and immorality. A young person who engages in illicit sexual activity is more spiritually vulnerable to other temptations as well.

HELPING THEM SAY NO!

If I were asked to name the number-one reason a child yields to sexual pressure, at the top of my list would be adolescent alienation brought on by parental inattentiveness. If you want to insulate your kids from the many sexual pressures, you must enter their world and connect with them through an open relationship of mutual respect and love. Establishing sexual prohibitions and rules without a nurturing, loving parent/youth bond often leads to relational disconnection and rebellion. But your rules and guidelines for sexual behavior offered within the context of an intimate relational connection will generally lead to a positive response. (Youth leaders, for further information on how you can discuss this subject with your students, see the book *Why Wait?*[5] and the video curriculum *No! The Positive Answer.*[6])

> Your rules and guidelines for sexual behavior offered within the context of an intimate relational connection will generally lead to a positive response.

The guidelines you do provide your young person in the context of relationships need to take the form of open communication about sex. Since our kids were very small, Dottie and I have talked very openly with them about sex. They grew up knowing they could ask any question and bring up any topic related to sex. We didn't act shocked. We didn't reprimand them for bringing up a forbidden subject. Discussions about sex with our kids were as normal as any other topic. We actually invited discussions on the topic and used movies, songs, TV commercials, etc., as opportunities to bring it up.

For example, when Katie was about twelve, I was driving her and a girlfriend somewhere in our van. I heard a lot of whispering in the backseat. Then Katie stuck her head up front and said, "Daddy, I have a question for you. What is oral sex?"

How would most parents respond to that question? Probably with shock. The question did take me by surprise, but I determined not to display any shock. Instead, I said, "Why do you ask, Katie?"

"Kids talk about it at school," she said, "so we want to know what it is."

I spent a few minutes appropriately explaining oral sex in terms the girls could understand, and it seemed to satisfy them. When I got home I called the other girl's mother, a single mom, and told her what I had done. I was a little nervous because I didn't know how she would respond to the news that I had informed her daughter about oral sex. Instead of being appalled, she was grateful, adding, "Thank goodness they asked *you* instead of me!"

The next day, Katie explained more about why she asked the question. "We were talking about it and I said, 'Let's ask my dad. I can ask him about anything.' She said, 'You can't ask him about *that*.' I said, 'Yes I can, and I'll prove it to you.'" I was grateful that Katie sensed that freedom, but I wasn't surprised, because we had cultivated openness on the topic in our family all along.

An open-door policy for talking about sex is no guarantee that your kids will remain morally pure. But it not only affords you the opportunity to explain sex from a godly perspective, it also lets them know you care about their perspective and understanding. Here are a few other suggestions for communicating about sex.

Use the proper terminology for body parts right from the beginning.

For example, call a penis a penis and a vagina a vagina; don't use any cute little terms. With all the sexual information circulating in our society, your children will hear the right terms anyway. They might as well learn from you what they are and what they mean.

Teach your kids respect for sex and the marriage relationship.

Respect is conveyed through the use of proper language for intercourse, not the slang or vulgarity kids will pick up if left to themselves to learn about sex.

Use day-to-day opportunities to talk about sex.

When your kids hear obscene words for sex or illegitimate sexual activity, take time to give them the proper terms and explain why the improper terms or activities are wrong. As stated previously, if a movie or TV show you see together glorifies illicit sex or other behaviors, take time to talk about God's view of sex in relationships.

The more open you are about sex at home, the less likely your kids will go outside the home to get information about sex. Arm yourself and your young person with the many reasons to say no to sexual pressure. Don't let him or her be the victim of ignorance, or allow them to be defenseless in the face of the pressure. And as you share God's loving perspective on sex, they will be able to sense your own loving heart to protect them from harm and to provide for their good—and that will help keep you relationally connected.

PART 4

The Faith Connection

CHAPTER 14

Connecting: Your Students' Faith and Future Depend on It

If you could wish anything for your children or for the young people you minister to week by week, what would you wish for? Do you think your aspirations for your kids would match up with their hopes and dreams? We surveyed more than thirty-seven hundred churched youth, asking them what they want out of life. You may find that their responses are very close to what you want for your kids. Here are the top five items kids said they wanted out of life, listed in order of priority:

1. Good physical health

2. One marriage partner for life

3. A clear purpose in life

4. Close, personal friendships

5. A close relationship with God[1]

If I had to summarize in one sentence what kids want, I would say they want a healthy and relationally meaningful life on earth and a home in heaven. And that's what we want for them too.

But as I stated in the first chapter of this book, countless numbers of parents, youth workers, and Christian leaders are running scared today because so many kids seem to be headed in the opposite direction. A godless culture threatens to undermine our young people's faith and moral character. Most adults are doing their best to protect their youth from the negative influences and consequences of a postmodern age. And I trust that in this book you have found positive, practical steps for insulating your kids against these negative influences by making six vital relational connections. Yet there is more to giving our kids what they want out of life than fortifying our loving relationship with them.

These six relational connections are foundational to the relationally meaningful life our children want to experience. By connecting with our kids, we give them a sense of authenticity, security, significance, lovability, importance, and responsibility. These elements are fundamental if our young people are going to have a clear purpose in life, a successful marriage, and enriching personal friendships. But what about our young people's faith in God and personal relationship with Him? Are solid relational connections on the horizontal level really vital to their vertical relationship with God?

Yes, your relationship with your students is vital to their faith in God. But you may be surprised—even shocked—to learn just how important you are to your students' developing a lasting, intimate relationship with God.

BELIEVING IS NOT ENOUGH

Recently, I began circulating a survey form to churched youth attending my speaking engagements. On this form, I ask questions that explore a young person's faith, such as: "Do you believe the Bible is totally accurate in all its teachings?"; "Do you believe Jesus Christ is the Son of God?"; and "Do you believe Jesus was crucified and literally rose from the dead?" I have already collected hundreds of these completed surveys.

I have been pleased to learn through my rather unscientific research that the vast majority of the churched youth who come to my meetings believe the fundamentals of the Christian faith—namely, the deity of Christ, His death and resurrection, and the reliability of Scripture. But I wanted to probe even deeper to determine how firm these students are in their beliefs. So during a recent youth conference, I decided to question Christian kids directly about their faith. The kids at this particular denominational conference had been handpicked by their church leaders. These were the denomination's brightest, most articulate, most mature, and most responsible young people—the cream of the crop, so to speak.

So at one point in the conference, I took a cordless microphone in my hand and stepped down from the platform. Wading into the crowd of beautiful, lively, and radiant young men and women, I started asking point-blank questions.

I held my Bible in the air and pointed the microphone at one student. "Do you believe the Bible is the Word of God?" I asked.

"Yes!" came the response with apparent confidence and conviction.

"Do you believe it is true?"

"Yes!" came the answer again.

Then I asked, "Why?"

Silence. No answer.

I thrust the microphone into another student's face, asking the same battery of questions.

"Yes!" came the answer every time.

"Why?"

Same response. Nothing.

And that's how it continued. The students answered the doctrinal part of the question with confidence and authority, but they couldn't answer why. Keep in mind, these were not little kids or new Christians. They were all young people from a strong evangelical denomination who had been involved in Sunday school, worship, youth activities, and Bible study. Many of them had been raised in Christian families, and they were regarded as among the finest Christian kids their generation has to offer. And while the apostle Paul admonished, "If you are asked about your Christian hope, always be ready to explain it" (1 Pet. 3:15 NLT), these kids couldn't. They were stumped.

The next day, a young man came to the morning session looking as though he was about to burst from excitement. He came up to me before the meeting started and almost shouted, "I know the answer!"

He caught me off-guard, and I wasn't sure what he meant. So I asked, "The answer to what?"

"To your question about why I believe the Bible is true and trustworthy."

"Okay," I said, "let's hear it."

"Because I believe," he answered with assurance. "Because I have faith."

"You're saying it's true because you believe it?"

"Yes!" He couldn't have sounded more convinced.

I looked around at the kids who had gathered to listen. Many of them were smiling and nodding their heads in agreement, as though this young man had solved a great riddle, and now it all seemed so obvious.

I then asked him, "Does this mean that the Bible would also be true for your neighbor or the kid down the street?"

"It would be if he believed it," the boy responded.

I gazed at him for a few seconds, then I said, "You know the basic difference between you and me?"

"What?" he asked, still smiling.

"To you the Bible is true because you believe it. I believe it because it is true."

Alarming as it may be, the fact is the majority of our young people today—even the brightest and best of them—believe that they are Christians *by the act of believing . . . period!* They have accepted a subjective believism that "if you believe it's right for you, then that's what makes it true for you." Our study of more than thirty-seven hundred churched youth reveals just what they do believe:

> The majority of our young people today—even the brightest and best of them—believe that they are Christians *by the act of believing . . . period!*

- Nearly half (46 percent) suspect that "it does not matter what religious faith you follow because all faiths teach similar lessons."

- Nearly half (48 percent) express either agreement or confusion as to whether "Muslims, Buddhists, Christians,
  Jews and all other people pray to the same God, even
  though they use different names for God."

- And an overwhelming 65 percent of our kids either
  believe or suspect there's no way to tell which religion is
  true![2]

Not surprisingly, those youth who state outright they don't
believe there is a truth that is right for everyone are twice as likely
to say that Satan is just a symbol of evil, twice as likely to say that
Jesus made mistakes, and almost three and one-half times more
likely to say that good works will earn you a place in heaven![3] It is
clear that Christ, to the majority of our kids, is *a* messiah—even a
good one—but not the true Messiah, the Savior to the whole world!

It is not enough for our kids to make a personal commitment
to Christ in which they merely believe Jesus is *a* messiah who is
their personal Savior. We must move
our young people beyond a subjective belief that says, "It's true
because I believe it," to an objective
faith that equips them to trust in
Christ and His Word because Christ
and His Word are true!

> Most young people
> who become Christians
> today do so not because
> they believe Christianity to
> be true or credible, but
> because they feel it is the
> best option they have
> found to date.

I am deeply concerned that the
vast majority of the young people
in today's Christian families and
churches are building their faith on
this false and changing foundation of
subjective belief. And because a subjective faith is unstable, the

"truth" they believe today can change tomorrow simply because their belief may change.

I am convinced that most young people who become Christians today do so not because they believe Christianity to be true or credible, but because they feel it is the best option they have found to date. They may be attracted to Christianity for a number of reasons: an exciting youth group, an emotional church-camp experience, the influence of a Christian friend, etc. But in many cases, it makes little difference to them whether the faith they embrace is factually accurate or true. And what's more, their "faith" is doing little to keep them from the consequences of wrong choices. I have also concluded that, unless our kids become convinced of the truth and credibility of their faith, when something more exciting or emotionally stimulating comes along, they will change their belief and abandon whatever Christian faith they do have.

TAKING THEM BEYOND BELIEF TO CONVICTIONS

A subjective belief does not need to be rooted in any basis of reality. It makes no difference whether what a person believes is reality or fantasy. The act of believing in and of itself makes something "right" for that person because truth is viewed as relative. But truth that is relative cannot be considered absolutely true or real.

Our young people need to develop convictions so they are convinced of the truth, rightness, and reality of Christianity. Our kids (and each of us) must be convinced of the truth with our hearts and our minds. I have often said the heart cannot rejoice in what the mind rejects. Our hearts will have a difficult time being convinced of something when our minds cannot confirm that it is true in reality. We need both our hearts *and* our minds to be convinced of the truth.

To move our young people from subjective believism to convictions that will hold them steady and firm in a godless culture, they need to *embrace a relational experience with Christ, the Person of Truth, so they believe in their hearts, and have a cognitive encounter with the evidence of that truth, so they can understand with their minds why they believe what they believe.* Our kids must become convinced in their hearts and minds of the truth, rightness, and reality of such fundamentals of the Christian faith as: (1) the deity of Christ, (2) His crucifixion, (3) His resurrection, and (4) the reliability of Scripture. When our kids are convinced in heart and mind that Christ and His Word are absolutely real and true, they will be able to resist temptation, be firm in their faith (see 1 Pet. 5:9), and testify of God's reality to the world around them with conviction.

> We need both our hearts and our minds to be convinced of the truth.

But here is the challenge we must face: "Truth" to the majority of our young people is whatever they believe it to be. So, even getting them interested in discovering the factual, evidential truth and reality of Christianity will be a challenge. Why should they be interested in examining, for example, the claims of Christ to be the one true God, when simply "believing" makes it true for them? Truth to our young people isn't something to be discovered as it was for previous generations; it is something to be created simply by believing it is true.

Our kids today have become very pragmatic. They want something that is relevant to their lives and relationships. As Andy

Crouch, an InterVarsity staff member at Harvard University, points out, "The . . . historical truth of a biblical book is not the burning issue [to today's youth], but rather how the Scripture speaks to their situation."[4] Our kids are no longer asking which faith is true or most credible, but which faith *works for them.* So to take our kids beyond subjective believism, we must not only show that Christianity works, but we must also show that it actively works *because it is true!*

THE RELATIONAL CONNECTION

Today's kids want something that is real to them. They want something that is relationally relevant to their lives. And while our kids may not be champing at the bit to know the evidences for a true faith in Christ and His Word, I believe they are desperately seeking a relational connection. As we have illustrated in this book, our kids want to know that someone cares for them and will *affirm them*—to identify with what they're going through so they can have a *sense of authenticity.* They need someone to make themselves *available* to them so that they can have a *sense of importance.* Our young people need someone to *accept them* for who they are so they can have a *sense of security.* They even want to be given boundaries and *be held accountable* so they can have a *sense of responsibility.* And when our kids lack that, they feel disconnected and alone.

In this book, we have tried to provide practical steps you can take to enter your students' world to make these connections. But what if I told you that the motivation your students need to examine the truth and reality of Christ and His Word is found in these very same relational connections? What if I could show you that God draws all of us to the truth, not just because of its evidential credibility, but also because of His compelling love as expressed in these relational connecting points?

Beginning in the spring of 2002, by God's grace, we will launch the Beyond Belief campaign, which will demonstrate that when the four foundational pillars of the faith (Christ's deity, His death, His resurrection, and the reliability of Scripture) are placed within a certain relational context, they become so relationally compelling that your kids will find them difficult to resist. I believe our kids will be relationally and spiritually gripped when they see these four powerful truths within the relational context of God making Himself available to them, affirming them, accepting them, and holding them lovingly accountable.

Merging Two Vital Tracks

For the past thirty years of my ministry, I have documented and presented the evidences of the Christian faith. My writing associates and I have published numerous books on solid reasons to believe. During this same period, we have written and spoken on the topic of relationships. We have published volumes for youth on love, sex, dating, and issues of right and wrong. Resources have been developed for adults on instilling biblical values of sexual morality in their youth and teaching them how to determine right from wrong.

In effect, I have traveled two separate ministry tracks during the years: one on evidences for the Christian faith and one on relationships. In the last couple of years, it has become clear that

God has led my ministry team and me to a message that merges these two tracks. And this is exactly what we will be doing in our next campaign.

The Beyond Belief campaign is designed to equip churches and families with a compelling relational context to instill rock-solid convictions of the Christian faith in their young people. This book, along with the companion PROJECT 911 family of resources, is the first step in providing relational context for the all-important process of passing on your faith. It is my prayer, and that of my entire ministry, that throughout the next decade we can serve you better.

This book and its companion PROJECT 911 resources serve as the foundation of the Beyond Belief Campaign. As we launch into the twenty-first century, I trust that our future ministry emphasis and resources will be able to serve you as never before to anchor the faith of your child or youth group in the reality of Jesus Christ. It is my prayer that as you connect with your youth and stay connected with them, you will be able to impart your life, your values, and your faith to them. As a result, they will both believe and live as "children of God without fault in a crooked and depraved generation, in which [they] shine like stars in the universe" (Phil. 2:15).

There is Truth, and we must tell the world about Him.

Since 1965, Josh McDowell has been telling the world the Truth about Jesus Christ.

The early years of Josh's ministry were spent primarily on university campuses speaking on behalf of Campus Crusade for Christ.

By the late '70s, with increasing requests to speak, Josh began publishing books and recording his talks on tape. He also began sharing his message internationally.

Today, the focus is still the same—to share God's Truth and challenge people to live their lives according to that Truth. But the "campus" has continued to expand.

The Josh McDowell Ministry reaches out to:

- *young people* in North America who are struggling to understand right from wrong and need to know why they believe what they believe, and the adults who care about them and work with them—as parents, pastors, educators, or youth workers

- *men, women, and children around the world* who want to know more about Jesus and are requesting millions of copies of Josh's books in their own languages

- *children and families in the former Soviet Union* who are suffering incredible hardships and need to be filled—both physically and spiritually

If you have any questions or would like more information about this ministry, please contact us:

Josh McDowell Ministry
Campus Crusade for Christ International
P.O. Box 131000
Dallas, Texas 75313
972-907-1000
www.josh.org

Appendix

More About Intimate Life Ministries

Several times in this book I have mentioned the work of David Ferguson. David's ministry has had such a profound effect on me in the past several years that I want you to have every opportunity to be exposed to his work and ministry. David and his wife, Teresa, direct a ministry called Intimate Life Ministries in Austin, Texas.

WHO AND WHAT IS INTIMATE LIFE MINISTRIES?

Intimate Life Ministries (ILM) is a training and resource ministry whose purpose is to *assist in the development of Great Commandment ministries worldwide.* Great Commandment ministries—ministries that help us love God and our neighbors—are ongoing ministries that deepen our intimacy with God and with others in marriage, family, and the church.

Intimate Life Ministries comprises:

- A network of *churches* seeking to fortify homes and communities with God's love;

- A network of *pastors and other ministry leaders* walking intimately with God and their families and seeking to live vulnerably before their people;

- A team of *accredited trainers* committed to helping churches establish ongoing Great Commandment ministries;

- A team of *professional associates* from ministry and other professional Christian backgrounds, assisting with research, training, and resource development;

- A team of *Christian broadcasters, publishers, media, and other affiliates,* cooperating to see marriages and families reclaimed as divine relationships;

- *Headquarters staff* providing strategic planning, coordination, and support.

How Can Intimate Life Ministries Serve You?

ILM's Intimate Life Network of Churches is an effective, ongoing support network for churches and Christian leaders. There are at least four ways ILM can serve you:

Ministering to Ministry Leaders

ILM offers a unique two-day "Galatians 6:6" retreat to ministers and their spouses for personal renewal and for reestablishing and affirming ministry and family priorities. The conference accommodations and meals are provided as a gift to ministry leaders by cosponsoring partners. Thirty to forty such retreats are held throughout the U.S. and Europe each year.

Partnering with Denominations and Other Ministries

Numerous denominations and ministries have partnered with ILM by "commissioning" them to equip their ministry leaders through the Galatians 6:6 retreats along with strategic training and ongoing resources. This unique partnership enables a denomination to use the expertise of ILM trainers and resources to perpetuate a movement of Great Commandment ministry at the local level. ILM also provides a crisis-support setting where denominations may send ministers, couples, or families who are struggling in their relationships.

Identifying, Training, and Equipping Lay Leaders

ILM is committed to helping the church equip its lay leaders through:

- *Sermon series* on several Great Commandment topics to help pastors communicate a vision for Great Commandment health as well as identify and cultivate a core lay leadership group.

- *Community training classes* that provide weekly or weekend training to church staff and lay leaders. Classes are delivered by Intimate Life trainers along with ILM video-assisted training, workbooks, and study courses.

- *One-day training conferences* on implementing Great Commandment ministry in the local church through marriage, parenting, or singles ministry. Conducted by Intimate Life trainers, these conferences are a great way to jump-start Great Commandment ministry in a local church.

Providing Advanced Training and Crisis Support

ILM conducts advanced training for both ministry staff and lay leaders through the Leadership Institute, focusing on relational ministry (marriage, parenting, families, singles, men, women, blended families, and counseling). The Enrichment Center provides support to relationships in crisis through Intensive Retreats for couples, families, and singles.

For more information on how you, your church, or your denomination can take advantage of the many services and resources, such as the Great Commandment Ministry Training Resource offered by Intimate Life Ministries, write or call:

Intimate Life Ministries
P.O. Box 201808
Austin, TX 78720-1808
1-800-881-8008
www.ilmministries.com

Notes

Chapter 1: The Disconnected Path of Self-Destruction

1. *USA Today*, 7 September 1999, 1D.
2. *New York Times*/CBS News poll of 1,038 youth ages thirteen to seventeen, as quoted in "School Rampages Possible," *Akron (Ohio) Beacon Journal*, 24 October 1999, B5.
3. John Leo, "When Life Imitates Video," *U.S. News and World Report*, 3 May 1999, 14.
4. Ibid., 14–15.
5. Josh McDowell and Bob Hostetler, *Right from Wrong* (Dallas: Word Publishing, 1994).
6. Rowland Nethaway, "Missing Core Values," Cox News Service, as quoted in *Hamilton (Ohio) Journal-News*, 3 November 1993.
7. Susan Mitchell, *The Official Guide to the Generations* (Washington, D.C.: U.S. Department of Education, Census Bureau, 1995), 12.
8. Barbara Kantrowitz and Pat Wingert, "How Well Do You Know Your Kid?" *Newsweek*, 10 May 1999, 38–39.
9. Study by Robert Kraut, professor at Carnegie Mellon University, as cited in "In Cyberspace," *Akron (Ohio) Beacon Journal*, 31 August 1998, "First Words" column, 1.
10. John Leland, "The Secret Life of Teens," *Newsweek*, 10 May 1999, 45.
11. Kantrowitz and Wingert, "How Well Do You Know Your Kid?", 38–39.
12. Mitchell, *The Official Guide to the Generations*, 12.

Chapter 2: The Relational Factor

1. Adapted from Josh McDowell and Ed Stewart, *My Friend Is Struggling with Conflicts with Others*, PROJECT 911 collection (Nashville: Word Publishing, 2000).
2. Shannon Brownlee, "Inside the Teen Brain," *U.S. News and World Report*, 9 August 1999, 47.

3. Ibid., 46–47.

4. Ibid., 45–54.

5. Quoted and drawn from Bruce Perry and John Marcellus, "The Impact of Abuse and Neglect on the Developing Brain," *Colleagues for Children* 7 (1997): 1–4.

6. Drawn from "The Brain: A Work in Progress—What We Know About It" from *Los Angeles Times* series, "The Brain: A Work in Progress," created by Internet *Web Edit* 7 November 1996.

7. Ibid.

8. Ibid.

9. Quoted and drawn from Perry and Marcellus, "The Impact of Abuse and Neglect on the Developing Brain," 1–4.

10. Sharon Begley, "Why the Young Kill," *Newsweek*, 3 May 1999, 35.

Chapter 3: Connecting Point #1: Affirmation—Giving Youth a Sense of Authenticity

1. Webster's New Collegiate Dictionary (Springfield, Mass.: G&C Merriam Co., 1975), 20.

2. Gloria Gaither and William J. Gaither, "I Am Loved" (Nashville: William J. Gaither, Inc., 1978). CCLI 14019.

Chapter 4: Connecting Point #2: Acceptance—Giving Youth a Sense of Security

1. Walter Bauer, *A Greek-English Lexicon of the New Testament,* trans. William F. Arndt, and F. Wilbur Gingrich (Chicago: University of Chicago Press, 1957), 874.

2. Josh McDowell, *Seeing Yourself as God Sees You* (Wheaton, Ill.: Tyndale House Publishers, 1999.

3. Charles Caldwell Ryrie, ed., *Ryrie Study Bible* (Chicago: Moody Press, 1976), 25.

Chapter 5: Connecting Point #3: Appreciation—Giving Youth a Sense of Significance

1. Kenneth Blanchard and Spencer Johnson, *The One Minute Manager* (New York: Berkeley Books, 1983).

Chapter 6: Connecting Point #4: Affection—Giving Youth a Sense of Lovability

1. L. Eisenberg, "Premature and Newborn," *Pediatrics* 103, no. 5 (May 1999): 1031–35.
2. David Ferguson, *The Great Commandment Principle* (Wheaton, Ill.: Tyndale House Publishers, 1998), 49–50.
3. M. J. Rutter, "Developmental catch-up, and deficit, following adoption after severe global early privation," *Child Psychiatry* 39 (1998): 465–76.
4. Kevin Leman, *Becoming the Parent God Wants You to Be* (Colorado Springs: NavPress Publishing Group, 1998), 86.
5. Adapted from Josh McDowell, *The Father Connection* (Nashville: Broadman and Holman Publishers, 1996), 4–6.
6. Louis O. Caldwell, *When Partners Become Parents* (Grand Rapids: Baker Book House, n.d.).
7. Claudia Wallis, "Stress: Can We Cope?" *Time,* 6 June 1983, 48–54.
8. Kathleen Fury, "Sex and the American Teenager," *Ladies Home Journal,* March 1986, 60.
9. Armand Nicholi Jr., "Changes in the American Family," *White House Paper,* 25 October 1984, 7–8.
10. McDowell and Hostetler, *Right from Wrong,* 255.

Chapter 7: Connecting Point #5: Availability—Giving Youth a Sense of Importance

1. 1994 Josh McDowell Churched Youth Study analysis, cited in McDowell and Hostetler, *Right from Wrong,* 259.
2. Ibid., 255–56.
3. *1999 Third Millennium Teens Research* (Ventura, Calif.: The Barna Research Group), 28.

Chapter 8: Connecting Point #6: Accountability—Giving Youth a Sense of Responsibility

1. Josh McDowell and Dick Day, *How to Be a Hero to Your Kids* (Dallas: Word Publishing, 1991), 188–206.
2. James Dobson, *Dare to Discipline* (Wheaton, Ill.: Tyndale House Publishers, 1970), 1–4.

Chapter 10: Connecting in Their World of Relational Losses

1. Adapted from Josh McDowell and Ed Stewart, *My Friend Is Struggling with the Loss of a Loved One*, PROJECT 911 collection (Nashville: Word Publishing, 2000).

Chapter 12: Connecting in Their World of Love and Sex

1. Adapted from Josh McDowell and Ed Stewart, *My Friend Is Struggling with Knowing True Love*, PROJECT 911 collection (Nashville: Word Publishing, 2000).

Chapter 13: Connecting in Their World of Sexual Pressure

1. Figures cited by Barna Research Group in *Baby Busters: The Disillusioned Generation* (Chicago: Northfield Publishing, 1994), 122–23.
2. Warren E. Leary, *New York Times*, 9 February 1989.
3. Josh McDowell and Bob Hostetler, *Josh McDowell's Handbook on Counseling Youth* (Dallas: Word Publishing, 1996), 281.
4. Nadine Brozan, "New Look at Fears of Children," *New York Times*, 2 May 1983, 85.
5. Josh McDowell and Dick Day, *Why Wait?* (Nashville: Thomas Nelson Publishers, 1987).
6. Josh McDowell, *No! The Positive Answer* video curriculum (Dallas: Word Publishing, 1993).

Chapter 14: Connecting: Your Students' Faith and Future Depend on It

1. McDowell and Hostetler, *Right from Wrong*, 261.
2. Ibid., 263.
3. Ibid., 312.
4. Quoted in Andres Tapia, "Reaching the First Post-Christian Generation," *Christianity Today* 38 (12 September 1994): 18–23.

FREE RESOURCE

Are you making the connection?

Do you want a closer relationship with your son or daughter? The youth in your church? Your students? Whether the children in your life are toddlers or teenagers, you want to understand them better. You want to be more involved in their lives and be prepared with godly wisdom and guidance when they need you.

The Josh McDowell Ministry wants to help. That's why we're offering a free pamphlet called "Make the Connection: Building a Better Relationship with Youth." In it you'll get a fun self-test for you and the children in your life to take to find out how connected you really are. You'll also find several recommendations for useful resources for building your relationship.

To request your *free* copy, simply fill out and return this reply form to: Josh McDowell Ministry, Campus Crusade for Christ, P.O. Box 131000, Dallas, Texas 75313.

[ ] Please send my free copy of *Make the Connection: Building a Better Relationship with Youth.*

Name_____

Address_____

City_____

State_____ ZIP_____

Phone_____/_____

E-mail_____

For Adults & Groups

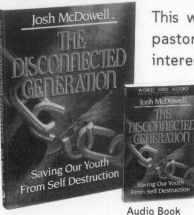

This watershed book is for parents, pastors, youth workers, or anyone interested in seeing youth not only survive but thrive in today's culture.

Audio Book

This book, directed specifically to fathers, offers ten qualities to form deepened relationships between dads and their kids.

Begin your church-wide emphasis with an adult group experience using this five-part video series. Josh provides biblical insights for relationally connecting with your youth.

Experience the Connection

Connecting Youth in Crisis

This PROJECT 911 Collection is eight small books, each dealing with a specific crisis that many youth encounter. Created in a fictional, though real-to-life format, the collection covers tough issues that often contribute to a young person's relational disconnect. These books employ a "read-it-and-give-it-away" strategy so you can offer "911 help" to a person struggling with one of these issues.

Experience the Connection

For Youth & Youth Groups

This eight-week youth group experience will teach your youth the true meaning of deepened friendships—being a 911 friend. Each lesson is built upon scriptural teachings that will both bond your group together and serve to draw others to Christ.

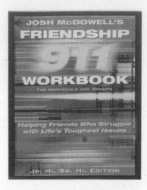

This optional video is an excellent supplement to your group's workbook experience.

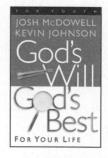

As follow-up to your youth group experience, continue a young person's friendship journey by introducing them to a thirty-day topical devotional journal and a book on discovering God's will in their life.

Experience the Connection

For Youth Workers

A one-on-one resource to help you provide a relational response and spiritual guidance to the 24 most troubling issues youth face today.

This handbook brings together over forty youth specialists to share their insights on what makes a successful youth ministry.

Contact your Christian supplier to obtain these PROJECT 911 resources and begin experiencing the connection God intended.